PANDEMIC PARODIES

The First 86 Days

Donna Hoffmeyer
Illustrations by Bianca Hoffmeyer

PANDEMIC PARODIES
The First 86 Days

ISBN: 979-8-9854734-0-7
First Edition: February 2022

Table of Contents

Preface

March 2020: The news was riddled with the start of the COVID-19 outbreak. We had just returned from an awesome Spring Break road trip that included visiting family in Bullhead, Arizona and Henderson Nevada, taking in the views of the Petrified Forest and Painted Desert along the way. It was the perfect pre-birthday gift. We felt fortunate to have this time, and even more so when everything started locking down.

March 16 became a day of "lasts" for me. It was the last day I was in the office before retiring; the last day I would make my morning commute; the last day I would wear my uniform. It was also the last day of our "normal life," at least for a while.

Novel Coronavirus-19 has, for the foreseeable future, changed the way we live our day-to-day lives. It's the only thing we hear about in the news. Needless to say, life has become pretty heavy lately. If there's anything life has taught me as a nurse, mom, teacher, trainer, and officer, it's that laughter eases stress.

I decided pretty quickly that we need to offset this heaviness with laughter. I wanted to offer people a distraction from everyday life, something they could read in the morning so they could start their day with a smile and a giggle.

On March 18th, I created *Pandemic Parodies* posts on Facebook, to capture the comical journey of my family's daily life during the COVID-19 pandemic. It was a hit among my family and friends. Over time, I decided to raise the bar, and donated to various non-profits based on how many likes, comments, and shares the post received—and in doing so, I forever captured moments we will be able to go back and laugh at years from now.

After 81 entries over 86 days, I put *Pandemic Parodies* to bed. I was nearing my transition out of the Air Force; things were getting extremely busy, and I truly thought COVID was winding down. (Little did I know how wrong I was.) Over the next two months, I was asked by various people if I was going to bring the posts back, or if I was considering putting these anecdotal stories in a book. After a couple weeks into terminal leave (using saved-up vacation time for all you civilians), I realized I was going to need a project. I definitely wasn't ready to job hunt, but I also knew I had to do something productive and fun. Bam! *Pandemic Parodies: The First 86 Days* was born.

There was one other reason I started the Parodies: It was a little lesson for me in vulnerability. I'm not overly comfortable with showing my hot-mess side... unless you're in my innermost circle. Blame it on my upbringing, personality, medical training, military training, or a combination of them all, but for me, being vulnerable was not a desired quality when I was in the midst of saving a life or prepping an aeromedical evacuation mission; nor is it something that was taught in any of my fields of work. Humor has always been a way for +me to diffuse frustration or ease a tense situation (I'd like to say when appropriate, but I miss that mark on occasion too). So, I thought this might be a good baby step in showing a little vulnerability.

These are mostly (90%) true stories of my family adventures of loving, laughing, coping, struggling, surviving, and thriving during the COVID19 Pandemic. The other 10% is *maybe* embellished for effect (e.g., comments on drinking; trust me, I may joke about it, but rarely do it. Heck, I'd be afraid of falling asleep and having the kids open the house for a rave.) ... or just that I forgot exactly how something happened. In any case, please enjoy.

Introduction

With each of my kiddos, I did a poop report on Facebook, because potty training is just a hysterical nightmare. Why not capture it?! Besides, it might give my kids a few tips for potty training their future minions. (This is, of course, me hoping there are grand-minions.) Might as well capture another major event... so here's the start of *Pandemic Parodies*.

Before we get started, you'll need to know the main players: my family.

Brian goes by many names—Dad, Daddy, Hoff, Hoffy, Bear, Big B, and The Big Guy. For this book, we're going to refer to him as TBG (The Big Guy). He earned those nicknames due to his 6'2" frame that fills a doorway. He is more reserved and observant in a crowd, a great conversationalist in a small group, and a total ham at home. He retired from the Air Force five years ago and works as a GS (Government Civilian) by day, adjunct instructor at night, student, amazing chef, amateur carpenter, avid hiker (when he can squeeze it in), volleyball champ (in his mind), and the glue that keeps everything going.

Brady (12, turning 13 at the time of this writing) is often referred to as Buddy, Brady Lee (usually in trouble), sometimes Brody (space-out moments; no offense to all the not-spacy Brodys in the world), but mostly just Brady. Coming in at 5 feet even, he's really excited he will soon be passing me in height. I remind him his wild hair gives him an extra inch. Lover of parkour, anime, Pokémon, ninja moves and video games, this kiddo is as sweet as they come. Often it appears he has no idea what's going on around him, but he amazes people when he's on point. He's full of obscure facts (did you know the platypus is the only mammal to lay eggs?) and always has a smile and a hug ready.

Bianca (8 turning 9, going on 29) is often referred to as B, Sassy Pants, Sassy, Baby Girl, and Bianca Grace (yep, trouble). I truly felt bad when we were pregnant with her. I was convinced she would be a shy, demure little girl, wondering how she got into this first-born family. Ha! Baby Girl tries to rule the roost. She's smart, astute, sassy, with an infectious giggle, and extremely organized. Definitely my Mini-Me (okay, minus the organized part). She loves creating, drawing, painting, singing, dancing, gymnastics, and now tennis. She is also the illustrator of this book. She collaborated with me, but everything in the book she drew herself. She wanted to tell a little about herself. So, here is Bianca...

"I like animals and I love my family, they're the best (some more than others). My favorite color is blue, and I want to be a zoologist and pilot when I grow up and work at the Columbus Zoo. (We're watching *Secrets of the Zoo* right now and it takes place at the Columbus Zoo. Heck, Mom wants to work there too!) I love my two dogs, cranky cat, and I want a Great Dane when I grow up."

Thank you, Bianca!

Amelia is our 13½-year-old mix breed mutt, referred to as Amelia Jane when she is in trouble, but it's worthless now that she's deaf. We just found out a few months ago she has cancer, but neither cancer nor deafness has stopped her sniffer from seeking out her favorite treats: food and tearing up a good toy.

Lilo is our 18-month-old Standard Poodle we inherited unexpectedly through a co-worker and friend; also referred to by her first and middle name when she is in trouble—Lilo Marley. She is a loveable hot mess. She always seems to know when one of us is in need of a cuddle with her soft curls. Fits in perfectly with the hot-mess family. Her favorite pastime is chasing our cat... Puck.

Puck's full name is Robin Goodfellow Puck (from *A Midsummer's Night Dream*) Hoffmeyer, or the cranky cat, but we just call him Puck. He has quite the attitude, likes TBG, tolerates the rest of us, and uses Lilo as his personal whipping post. He spends most of his time in the garage right now (we'll get to that story later).

I guess that leaves me: Mom, Mommy, Hey Mom, No Mom, and Mommmmm are the most common names I seem to go by lately. Donna, Babe, Boss and CINCHOUSE are TBG's terms of endearment for me. I have no doubt there are others when we aren't seeing eye-to-eye. I'm soon to be retired from the military. One month, three days to be precise. This is an enormous transition: going from throttle to I'm not sure exactly what. That appears to be the question. Fortunately, we planned my retirement so that I could choose if I wanted to go back or not. Right now, it's full-time Mom, remote schooler extraordinaire (big difference from homeschooler extraordinaire), in between everything, author, and searcher for myself. The last one might take a while.

All righty: you have a little background on the Hoffmeyer clan. Let's get on with the *Pandemic Parodies*.

DAY 1
March 16, 2020

Novel Coronavirus-19 is not just *in* the news, it is the *only* news. We can't turn on the radio, TV, or Internet without hearing about it. The deluge of information, coupled with just coming back from vacation, is throwing me into input overload. We're all still trying to process what the impact will be. Right now, all we know is the kids are remote learning, I'm still going to work, and The Big Guy has been sent home to telework.

First day of working from home for TBG. He's excited to accomplish his long to-do list, including building a standing desk. I'm not sure he fully realizes he's teleworking *and* watching kids today. But who am I to say? He'll probably have everything humming.

I end up leaving work early today because I'm not feeling well, and come home to a very frustrated guy. He got nothing done. For a guy who can complete multiple tasks in a day, he's nearly losing his mind. I don't feel bad, I feel vindicated! I'm lucky if I accomplish a task, much less remember what task I was *trying* to accomplish. Welcome to my world, Babe.

On a serious note, we both quickly realize we need a schedule.

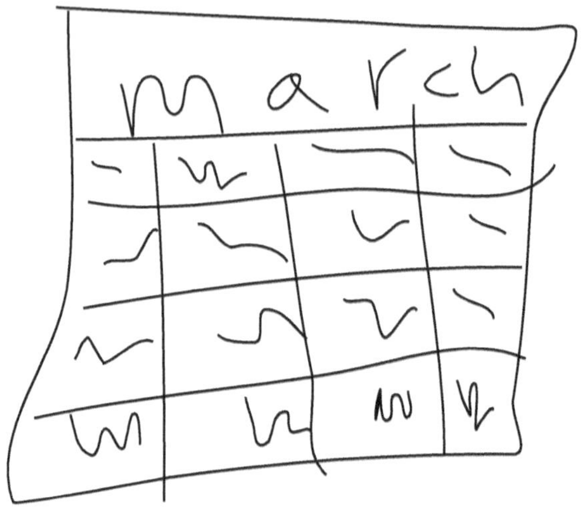

DAY 2
March 17, 2020 (My Birthday)

First day of "homeschooling" (and my birthday... WTH). Randolph School District flipped their classes to online nearly overnight. Needless to say, it is utter chaos. Teachers are making it up as they go along, and students are lost trying to follow the teachers, who are doing their best to navigate in the dark. Parents are basically stuck watching a comedy of errors (no fault of the school), and trying to figure out where to interject to help the situation. I decided the best way to handle all of this is with grace, understanding, and laughter (with the occasional eye roll).

But let's talk about the REAL crisis here: my hijacked birthday.

I am not the kind of person to have the birthday month, week or even weekend (not that I would mind, I just don't put the effort in.) However, I do enjoy a day of celebrating another successful trip around the sun. A few gifts, dinner out, and maybe an hour to read a book or take a nap. This is definitely *not* my idea of an awesome birthday, for the simple fact that my options were taken away from me. I'll suck it up (like I have a choice) and focus on the positive. I'll remain thankful for the flowers, bag of chocolate, and the big smiley faces giving me those gifts. I'm counting my blessings:

Day 2

educational apps; a child who can play his clarinet without sounding like a tortured mouse; and friends who know birthday cake solves all problems (thank you, Kathy Morrison). I'm reminding myself to be grateful for the awesome road trip we took over Spring Break, because my gut is telling me it may be a lonnnnng while before we get to go on another one... and I am NOT reminding myself my birthday is landing on the first day of involuntary homeschooling due to a pandemic. It's about the best I can do.

DAY 3
March 18, 2020

TBG scrapped his idea for making a standing desk. Instead, we have a large moving box with a wooden plank functioning as a modified standing desk. Granted, it's creative, but it's also an eyesore. Ahh well, it meets the need for right now. In our more "mature" age, neither of us can handle sitting for long periods of time. TBG's back and my hips start to ache. Oh, 40s, how we have fought with you this decade! Way before the Vari desk was ever a "thing," TBG built us standing desks. My office was so enamored with his work that TBG went into small production, outfitting a few of my workmates with a Hoffmeyer original. They are too big to drag back to the house, and we really don't have a place to put them. Ghetto moving-box desk it is!

One of the neighborhood kids knocks on the door at 0830 (seriously... don't they have school?). After rolling out of bed at 0845 (they rarely sleep that late), the kids get down to homework. They rock it out until 2 PM. I'm caught up in three telecons, so TBG is holding down the fort (which includes a nap during "science"... thank you, Bill Nye the Science Guy). PE consisted of water-gun fights with the neighborhood kids... at six feet apart. Bet they never had Nerf wars for gym time before! Only two more days, three telecoms, and tag-team homeschooling this week...we got this!

Vert

DAY 4
March 19, 2020

I'm trying to establish some normalcy during all this chaos. First step: get out of bed. I drag myself out of bed at 0615 with Mr. Sunshine and walk the dogs. Someone please explain to me how you pop out of bed VOLUNTARILY before the sun rises. Even though I'm not a morning person, I appreciate the early morning quiet. It's just that transition from a warm bed to the cold air I find challenging. God only knows, once the wild ones are up, there is ZERO quiet; nor is there any quiet place to hide right now. I fear this could become an issue in another month.

Fortunately, the kids have decided this would be a perfect time to have a growth spurt and sleep in again until 0845 (two days in a row!), then proceed to request a five-course breakfast. Much to Bianca's sadness, Dad makes French toast with the leftover French baguette from last night.

Bianca, crinkling her nose, says, "It's too eggy."

TBG gives her a big smile. "Too bad... enjoy!"

Bianca, left with zero options, chokes a piece down. Amazing what happens when you're really hungry.

It's going to be a great day! Only one telecon for me. (I find it sad that I'm measuring my work happiness by the number of telecons I have in a day.) The kids start homework ON THEIR OWN (another thing that never happens), then take a break and wipe down the surfaces and doorknobs ON THEIR OWN (holy Twilight Zone!). They go back and work a little more on their homework, and then head outside to get a little raking on. I'm thinking to myself, "We got this!"

Ha! Definitely thought too soon. We don't got this.

At 1305, 30 minutes prior to my ONLY telecon (but a very significant one), TBG decides he has to run to the office. At precisely 1306, the kids decide to argue over who has cleaned up the most dog poop and raked the most leaves.

Brady, all frustrated, says, "Bianca, I am always picking up most of the dog poop. You always walk around the area they never poop!"

Bianca, all angry: "I'm cleaning the poop too!"

Brady, shaking his head, "Yeah, barely, and you don't want to rake, but you want to jump in the leaves."

At this point, I am starting to lose my mind; my computer is jacked up, they're arguing, and I'm breaking out in a sweat, seeing as I have to be ready to go in less than 10 minutes. Did I mention I haven't had a chance to look over the slides I need to brief? Like any normal multitasking mom, I'm trying to unscrew my computer while lecturing the kids on stupid arguments. It's not going so well. So I decide at this point, I need the win-win. I stop the raking, turn the TV on, and like bugs to a light, they immediately sit down and zone out (hey, *Who Was* is educational... don't judge). I'm soon racing upstairs, praying my computer fixed itself. At precisely 1329, I call in for my telecon briefing. Yeah, I got this.

TBG comes home and sends the kids back outside for more slave labor (not really... food is payment, right?). Once he gets them on track, raking and poop collection is completed...and to add a cherry to the top, food comes to our door tonight! I totally forgot we ordered a trial of Hello Fresh. Score! Well, minus the fact that I have to actually cook it. This would be so much better if it came with a cute chef. But hey, at the end of the day, we have a family meal and Brady chows it down. (This may also have something to do with the fact we forgot lunch today... oops.)

We're trying to get our kiddos into a bedtime routine that includes a shower every night. Up until now, we would wrangle them into the shower every other night. (I know, it was a "picking our battles" situation.) Enter COVID, muahahahaha; there are a few benefits to this nasty virus. We just leveraged the situation to our advantage to get them to the shower every night without a fight. Trust me, it's not perfect.

Our youngest child is adamant she took a shower. TBG takes a look at her. Yes, her hair is wet, but she doesn't smell any better. "Bianca, I see you're wet, but you don't have that fresh soap smell. Unless we have fungus-scented shampoo and body wash, I'm guessing you didn't really take a shower."

"Dad, I took a shower!"

"Fair enough, but I'm sending you back to use soap this time."

"Hmrph." She stomps up each step in an effort to get her displeasure across to us.

Later that night, I decide a hot shower would be nice. I'm a little achy and slightly tense from trying to juggle kids, remote learning,

and my job. What I get is barely a lukewarm one. There's nothing like shaving goosebumps. I'm now regretting TBG sending Bianca back for a second go.

We finally get everyone tucked in. Fifteen minutes later, the eldest said child has decided he can't sleep and comes down to have a cup of tea. Yes, we have a 12-year-old tea connoisseur. He makes himself a cup and proceeds to question us on how the Seven Wonders of the World were created.

Well, we survived another day. Tomorrow might be a little concerning, because we ate the rest of the cake tonight.

DAY 5
March 20, 2020
(First day without cake)

Did I mention we have no more cake?

My "day" started at 2300 the night before, when my salivary glands went into hyperdrive. I now feel like I have Niagara Falls running down the back of my throat, causing me to cough until I dry heave. At this point, TBG is deciding if he should call the COVID19 team and have me taken away, or just put me out of my misery himself.

An hour later, I finally settle down and start to peacefully drift off, only to be awakened by a little Cindy Lou Who voice. "Mommy?" (Is it too late to change my name?) She can't sleep... "my 'who-ha' (privates) hurts." Translation, I'm anxious and I know you'll fall for this. Don't get me wrong; there has been validity in the past, and an Epsom salts bath seems to ease it. Recently, she hasn't seemed to have any issues; her little girl parts have not been red, yet she still complained. Like I said before, I usually appease her with an Epsom salts bath for 10 minutes. However, last night there was a pretty nasty lightning storm. I decided we have enough issues right now, and tell her to climb in bed. Amazingly, sleeping between Mom and Dad is a cure for a hurting who-ha. Who knew!?

Now I can't sleep, because I am trying to balance myself on the edge of one side of the bed, TBG is doing the same on the other,

and the tiny one somehow managed to Elasti-Girl herself across the entire bed. Niagara Falls starts again.

I give up at 5 AM and crawl downstairs onto one of the couches and finally pass out. TBG finally gives in at 6:00 and gets up, walks the dogs, and lets me sleep. I'm sure he was totally endeared by a runny-nose, tissue-holding hot mess. This is marriage at its finest, folks.

I creak open an eye at 1025. Dammit, kind of have that whole telework thing to do... thanks, Babe. As luck would have it, my computer wouldn't connect online all freaking day. Somehow, the day sped by, and at 4:00 in the afternoon, I found myself still in my pjs, wild hair and all. "Well hell, I'm just ready for bed a little early...whatever."

At 5:00, I finally connect and feel compelled to work for a couple hours to make up for the day. It also helps that I have zero interest in watching the kids' movie pick, *Super Jam.* (I do wonder if I will ever see a movie rated above PG13 again.)

I remind myself to look on the positive. Today, we didn't forget to feed the kids lunch. SCORE! TGIF!

Day 5

DAY 6
March 21, 2020

I slept! Didn't hack until 8 AM. I'm sure two children were wildly excited that they didn't have to deal with a sleep-deprived crazy lady. TBG and I have a game plan to keep the wee ones entertained. But before we implement Operation Wear Them Out, I decide a hot bath would be good to open me up a little. I have a small arsenal of essential oils. I figured it can't hurt to add a few to the bath: a little rosemary, a little sage, a little peppermint. "Ooooh, garlic, just three little drops should kill something. I'll add more lemon and peppermint to cover the smell." Pretty proud of myself for the think-through.

WHATEVER! TBG comes upstairs and thinks I'm bathing in garlic bread. Bianca wants to know why I'm cooking Italian food upstairs. The dogs are trying to find the hidden food, and my backside looks like it has chemical burns. (Which might explain why I felt like my skin was sloughing off in the tub.) Okay, bad choice. On the bright side, now I know how to get alone time.

Time to get the day going. Bianca decides she's going to make a get-well cake for our neighbor's daughter. I'll back-track a little here.

We have a trampoline for the kids to practice their flips, and often the neighborhood kids come over to jump. I try to keep an eye out and manage the madness to mitigate the risk of injury. Last week, a few of the kids were at the house jumping. Bianca comes running in and hollers, "Mom, R. hurt her ankle on the trampoline."

"What do you mean by *hurt*? Is she bleeding?" I'm a nurse; "hurt" is quantifiable, from "needs a second to shake it off" to "call the ambulance."

"No, she was jumping and her foot landed on the side of the trampoline, on the bar part."

I go out and take a look. R. is sitting in the jake (wooden) chair with her foot up on the outdoor table. She's not crying or upset, but her ankle looks the size of a small clementine.

"R., does it hurt?" I ask her as I move her foot, feeling around for any signs there may be a break.

"Yes," she says, now looking a little sad.

I ask TBG to carry her down to her house, and I text her parents. Fortunately, they are understanding and have a similar belief of kids being kids. The next day, I text her Dad to see how she is doing. They ended up going to Urgent Care, and it turns out she had a broken ankle. I asked it if it was a hairline fracture, because there was nothing obvious when I examined her ankle. Sigh of relief when he said it was. I was beginning to think I was losing my skills.

When I tell the kids, they feel bad.

Today, Bianca pipes up, "I'm going to make R. a cake and decorate it myself!"

I have visions of a kitchen full of frosting and sprinkles. "Okay, let's see what we need to get."

Brady and Brian are modifying a Nerf gun. They started looking up how to turn a Nerf gun into a semi-automatic and automatic Nerf.

I've warned them it had better not cause any trips to the emergency room or Urgent Care. They both just smirked at me.

Five hours and two worn-out parents later, we have cake batter, fondant, frosting, glitter, Nerf guns, and soldering equipment strewn across the kitchen and family room... with a pink glittery cake, automatic Nerf gun (warning was not heeded; that damn thing hurts) and two happy, slightly sugar-high kids.

In the midst of our cake-making/Nerf modifying event, we're sad to see in the headlines that Kenny Rogers has passed away. It really didn't matter what genre of music you listened to; everyone knew the song *The Gambler.* We decide to pay tribute to the legend with a movie ode to Kenny Rogers, *Six Pack.* Not sure if they truly like it, but when you're told this is the show of the evening and you have limited electronic time (and are a technology addict), you get your fix any way you can.

Day 6

DAY 7
March 22, 2020

The minions have decided they need another pet, because two dogs and a cat are not enough. They both put a lot of "thought energy" into this, and had their arguments prepared.

Bianca is the first to pipe up. "Mom, Brady and I decided we want a pet of our own." Before I can take a breath, she raises up her hands in a "hold up" motion. "Hear me out, Mom. The dogs follow you around and the cat only likes Dad. So, really we don't have our own pet."

We decide to entertain this a bit longer.

Bianca continues, "We want a hamster, gerbil, or rat, and we've been researching them." Brady is nodding his head in agreement, with a big old grin on his face non-verbally saying, "Oh yeah, we got this!"

Okay, we're a little impressed with the proactiveness. Why can't they be that way with homework and chores?

TBG rebuts, "Don't you think Puck (cat) would try to eat them?"

This causes them to ponder, until stupid Mom chimes in with, "You'd need an enclosed system with tubing that ran from one room to the next." Two sets of eyes light up like lottery machines hitting Jackpot. TBG is so not impressed with me right now.

Fortunately, TBG keeps the conversation moving along. "This is going to be a lot of work to upkeep." (Nice save, Big Guy.) Oh, but they are relentless and savvy.

Day 7

"How about fish?" Brady offers up. Ugh, the only thing we're good at with fish is killing them. However, Dad uses this as ammo. He's willing to entertain the idea, under one condition. "You guys have to start independently caring for our current pets now."

Say what?! My inside voice says, *"Where in God's name are we going to put a fish tank? They better be thinking of digging a koi pond in the backyard. Our cat can open closed doors and open up the dog food bags... ummm, yeah, a fish tank will be child's play."* I'm foreseeing future disasters. For an instant I am thankful for COVID19, because I'm pretty sure the pet store isn't open right now. Whether it is or isn't, we're using COVID as our excuse.

The rest of the day is spent trying to figure out where our lovely littles found the crack. Sheesh, they're W.I.L.D. Two rainy days in a row will do that. Trying to be responsible parents (keyword *trying*) and get everything ready for remote learning tomorrow, while they swing off chandeliers, is legal grounds to start drinking. We give up, and instead chose to feed them and take them out for a walk. Sigh, just to get them out the door for the walk is like trying to herd wet cats on speed. Where one is, the other is not.

"I forgot my shoes."

"How far do we have to walk?"

"Can I get water?"

"Can I take my scooter?" (No.)

I think the walk wears us out more than them.

As bedtime approaches, we're pumping them up for a fun day of school at home tomorrow. "It's going to be a great day tomorrow! We'll have fun!" Pretty sure we're convincing ourselves more than them.

Well, that's met with mixed emotions. Brady starts crying and says home is where he gets away from school (specifically, when he gets to go out to play). We get it, and of course feel bad. However, we know better than to feed that beast. So, we do what any tough-love parents would; we nicely say, "Suck it up, buttercup, you'll make it."

Bianca, on the other hand, comes down in the morning with a "business suit" on (shirt with a ruffle and a brown flowered skirt) and a briefcase (her portable art supplies) in hand; requests we have her workspace set up for her tonight; and is so beyond excited, I'm not sure if we're starting school or I lost track of time and it's Christmas tomorrow (southern Texas, folks... it's easy to be confused). We tuck her in and she hands us a note to read before we start tomorrow.

Dear Miss and Mr. hoffmeyer,

Can I bring my little red notebook in case I need scrap paper to solve and erase? About the seating chart, will I be at the table and Brady at the card table or the other way around?

Sorry, can I call you Miss and Mr Hoffmeyer or just Mom and Dad?

Can I bring a spar(e) book just in case and can I bring Lenny? (her lamb.)

Thank you!

I'm trying to figure out how we're going to be able to keep up with her when she becomes a teen.

After a busy day and kids in bed, TBG decides to make us a hot toddy. Great idea! We need it. Apparently this concoction has whiskey, honey, and lemon. Well, I can taste one out of three, so sleep should come easy tonight.

DAY 8
March 23, 2020
(Remote Learning Day 1)

Woot woot! Let the homeschooling begin! We've already worked with the kids setting up schedules in their planner, making sure the wee one could access her online classroom, let them pick breakfast for the next day (oatmeal), and *The Sound of Music* was playing in our heads as we got them to bed. The Big Guy and I thought we were all prepped for today. Oh, how so, so wrong we were.

We decide to let them sleep until they wake (Mistake #1). At approximately 8 AM two starving kids come down the stairs to see Mom in her new home fashion: pjs, make-up free and wild hair. In my defense, I hacked up at least half my lung lobes last night... damn post-nasal drip. We start to get work going (Mistake #2).

Bianca is ready to rock and roll with her schoolwork. "Hold tight, Bianca. You need to eat a good breakfast first. I made oatmeal for you." (Okay, the Instapot did, but someone had to throw it in there and push buttons.)

Okay, let's rock and roll! Everything is starting off pretty well. Both kids are working on assignments; we're getting our telework on. We got this!

Four hours later...

Whoever said, "We got this!" needs to be shot.

At 1300, TBG is going out to do a last apocalypse run (sans the hot commodity, toilet paper), pick up Brady's meds from school, hit the Commissary (grocery store for all you civilians), drop off paperwork, and be back home in record time. (Mistake #3 for even thinking this). "Any last requests? This is the last run for a few weeks."

I immediately blurt out, "Yes! Chocolate!" I figure it's probably what will be keeping us (me) sane for the next couple weeks.

TBG leaves for the final outing. The kids are entertaining themselves; I'm on the phone with work. We're good, right? Wrong. Five freaking minutes after the door closes, Bianca is yelling at

Brady, he's walking upstairs crying, and I'm on the phone wondering what the hell just happened. All that's going through my head is *How in the name of God can my dear husband time his exits so damn perfectly?*

Now I have one overwhelmed kiddo (ADHD is a bi@$ch some days). I give him 15 minutes to regroup; still have no idea what happened. At this point, I don't care why, I just want calm. Like magic, down the stairs he comes, smiling again. Alrighty, let's keep going. He has a group meet with his math teacher next. He puts on his headset and is listening. Bianca is working away. The balance is restored.

Okay, I'm going to set the stage a little for the next sequence of events. Throughout the day, the kids ask me to come over for help. They ask questions, and I start to answer or get on their computer, only to be met with... "Wait, Mom," an eye roll, or "You don't get it." Excuse me, but *you* are asking *me*! Apparently *you* aren't getting it... and if I'm not and you're not, then who the hell is? Needless to say, it's been a bit frustrating. Okay, I'll admit it... it's been EXTREMELY frustrating. Let's add that I haven't been able to focus on my work for most of the day.

Okay, back to the story.

Brady calls me over because Zoom is freezing up. I walk over and start to look at the computer, and little do I realize he's panicking over missing some of the discussion, and he just starts pushing buttons and telling me to wait. Out of frustration and before I can catch myself, something to the effect of, "Grrrr... you are being a pain in my a$% right now!" might have slipped out. Lesson #50000 on remote learning: always check the mute button BEFORE speaking. I watched Brady's eyes grow to the size of saucers, his mouth slowly opening in disbelief.

"Mom, the picture is frozen, not the audio!" Brady begins to cry, slams his computer closed (thank you, baby Jesus), and absolutely breaks down, thinking of the embarrassment of his Mom swearing on his Math class group meet. I'll be honest, I wasn't thinking much of his embarrassment, I was thinking of mine. Exactly how am I going to explain this to the teacher?

TBG is home (yes, he got chocolate) and at this point is smirking, shaking his head, and only keeping in the hysterical laughter because our kid is in tears. Jerkface.

Well, the day officially went to hell. TBG and I realize we need a new game plan. We salvage what we can with a family dinner, evening walk, game of Life, and an apology email to the teacher. Lucky for both of us, she said too many people were talking at once to be able to hear anything. I personally think she was giving me a little grace and understanding to save face. I'll take it.

My Karma tonight is trying to get work done late at night and watching my Outlook sit and spin, going nowhere fast... serves me right.

Whelp, really not looking to out-do myself tomorrow. Hitting the reset button... wish us luck!

DAY 9
March 24, 2020

Everyone's ready to rock and roll! TBG and I wiggle telecons in between helping the kids. He starts helping the kiddos get situated and I start getting systems operating. Only problem is, they (as in systems, not children) don't want to (can't say I blame them). So, while I'm waiting for the blue circle of death to unscrew itself, I figure I can jump in and help the kids. Apparently, I was soooooo wrong. When Bianca comes to ask me a question, TBG stops her mid-sentence. "Hey, I'm the teacher this morning. What do you need?" Both of us just look at him, wondering where Mr. Rogers came from. Oookay, I'll go back to staring at my non-functioning computer and send texts to folks expecting things from me.

At 9:25 I'm "allowed" (please read that with a snarky tone for proper effect) to oversee the kids' learning. TBG scoots upstairs for his telecon, I start helping Brady with his work, and 25 minutes later I get a text from a co-worker that she just dialed in for the telecon. What telecon? Ummm, yeah, all over that. No computer functioning means no calendar sending me those "Hellur, Swiss Cheese Brain, you have a meeting" reminders. I quickly text and ask for the phone number/passcode. No luck; the meeting had already started and she didn't see the text. Really hope this isn't a meeting day, and if it is, I really hope I can remain blissfully ignorant and claim plausible denial.

We all stop for a break around 11:00. Brady has to get his seven-minute PE workout requirement done. Seven minutes! That's it?

Day 9

What exactly is the goal here, to get them in shape or just avoid blood clots from sitting all day? (And we wonder why kids have no stamina these days.) Bianca and I decide to jump in and work out with him.

I'm going to preface this with the fact that I have a Master's in

sports science, and I am a bit of a form freak. Ahhh, my children, they can run around playing with friends for hours, but look like a crippled Richard Simmons doing a basic seven-minute workout. Let's call it what it really is... a warm-up.

"Brady, your hands go above your head when you do a jumping jack."

"Bianca, it's called a plank, not a Humpback Whale."

"Brady, you have to actually bend your arms to call it a push-up."

"Yes Bianca, it *is* cool you can stand on one foot while you stretch... no. I'm not attempting it."

Pretty sure it ended up being a 3.5 min workout.

I gave up on my computer functioning and decided on listening to one of Bianca's stories read online by the comedian Wanda Sykes.

If any of you know of her, you know exactly why I am listening. She is hilarious! She also renews my faith in keeping sane with a little witty humor.

We survive the day with only one small meltdown from Brady. I'd call that success! With our tiny bit of confidence built, we get an email stating they are extending remote school to 24 April. Poof, confidence deflated. We're deciding if it's too early to start day-drinking.

While we're making dinner, I look over at our puppy Lilo (60 lbs of standard poodle awesomeness), trying to look at us under her black mop. First available appointment at the groomers was 22 April. Well, damn.. .it's looking like it's going to be a DIY. I mention to TBG we're going to have to figure out how to give her a trim this weekend. To which he and Brady light up and TBG says, "Yeah, Brady and I are going to give her a Mohawk!" At this point, I am hoping his bad idea

doesn't spark further stupid ideas, and praying the kids don't remember we have colored hair wax. Stay tuned for the upcoming "Hey Mom, Watch This," event.

As we're settling down for the evening, I mention to TBG that as this pandemic is ramping up, the Reserves are gathering data on their medical personnel. I thought it was smart for us to be aware of what the future might hold. He smirked at me and said, "Now listen, if you have to go, you better be extremely careful" (married almost 14 years, I know what is coming next), "because there is no way you're going to leave me as a single dad to homeschool and raise these Wild Kratts by myself!" (Bazinga!) Nothing like a guy with his priorities straight.

DAY 10
March 25, 2020

Sweet baby Jesus, we barely survived today.

The morning started off as normal (if there is such a thing). I ask the kids how they slept. Brady, eating the first of 10 meals today, pipes up, "Good! Well, until my fart woke me up last night. Did you hear me wake up?"

"Ummm... thankfully, I didn't hear it or smell it." Looking on the bright side, I know there's no chance COVID-19 could survive in his room.

I know better than to ask TBG how he slept. My post-nasal drip has slowed down considerably, but I swear the one little drip it does every 20 minutes has laser beam accuracy for triggering my cough reflex, and I sound like an 80-year-old smoker. Needless to say, he was not thrilled to be the involuntary audience for my cacophony, and kept rolling the sheets around like an alligator in a death roll.

We get the morning going, and the kids jump into their work. I, amazingly, get in my email for all of about 30 minutes. The VPN trolls decide I'm done and kick me off for the rest of the day. TBG is in a similar situation, so we give up until the evening and pitch in with homeschooling.

In a matter of a few hours, Brady's workload somehow magically increases and all of a sudden the to-do list exponentially grows. His poor little ADHD brain nearly explodes. Let the meltdowns begin (ours and his). If you haven't used Google Classroom, you're missing out. It's like playing Find the Assignment. It could be in the communication thread, or the classroom tab, calendar, or listed on the overview. Who knows? Each of the seven teachers has their own way. This isn't bagging on our teachers. They've busted butt to move to online teaching. It's just a fact that the learning curve is steep, and even steeper for the parents of a child whose organizational skills match those of Tigger on crack.

So it's Wednesday, and Brady has 30 social study questions for today and a paper due tomorrow. Good deal; he should be done with both today. Okay, let me rephrase that... we are *hoping* he'll be able to have both done today. Sometimes we really underestimate the power of a distracted mind. Four painful hours later, he turns in his 30 questions. Sweet Mama, we still have a paper to finish. At the same time, TBG is helping Bianca and finds she had a paper she was supposed to have started on Monday and we overlooked. We look at each other and do what any overwhelmed parents do... send the kids out to play and take a damn break.

I'm frustrated, and TBG is the same. He decides he's going to step out for a few to go get sunflower seeds at Walmart. I have the wife "Have You Done Lost Your Mind?" look on my face, and he proceeds to receive the nursing, COVID, have-you-not-listened-to-CDC-guidance-and-you-will-not-die-without-sunflower-seeds lecture. Escape bubble busted.

"I think a form of prenuptial should be signed where divorce is not allowed during homeschooling. If, after homeschooling is complete, the couple still wants to divorce, then fair game."

"I'm not sure I could do that because, you know, I'm a hot commodity," he says with a smirk. Two of my close girlfriends have asked to clone him, and now he thinks he's The Most Interesting Guy.

Now that TBG realizes he isn't going anywhere, we both agree we'll each help out with a paper. Translation: they talk, we type. At this point, I'm thinking it would have been nice if they'd have skipped all the handwriting in preschool and went right to typing.

Kids, now fed and aired out, are ready to start again. About an hour in, I get a message from the Science teacher on Remind (yet another app to master) to remind the kids to read four chapters, answer questions, check in here, finish a project, and who the hell knows what else—and have it done by Friday. WTH! Where the hell was all this hidden? I can't find it; neither can TBG. It was a major struggle, but I managed to send a nice email. Fortunately, we get a quick response back. Sure enough, the information was in the classroom tab. Well hells bells, ya could have sent that reminder on Monday, not Wednesday!

Meltdown #5 ensues.

We manage to get through dinner and get them outside for a little bit. Brady still hasn't finished his paper, and with the surprise extra work we have to push him to the paper finish line. We coax him back in to take shower, feed him (meal #9) and get back to this godforsaken paper.

He needs 500 words on the history of the clarinet. He has 498. TBG is pretty much done. "Close enough, Brady."

Brady not missing a beat, "It would be sad if you make me fail, Dad." Gut punch to Dad. Mom's years as both a college grad and adjunct faculty came through in the clutch. "Brady, put THE END." Problem solved.

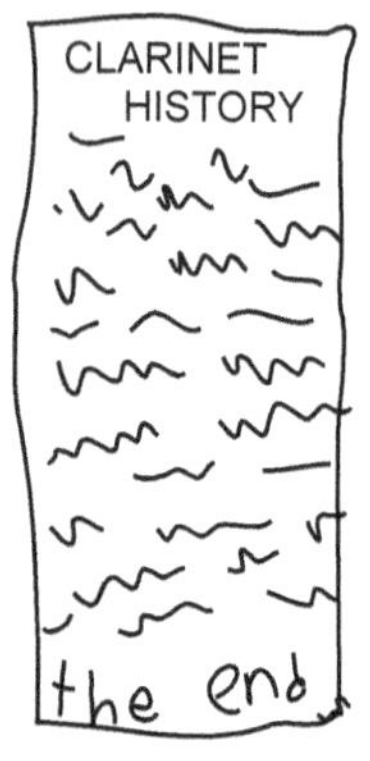

I need to recap so y'all can get the picture at the end of the night. This kid proudly told me his farting awake story, could hardly stay on track throughout the day, and had a meltdown at managing the volume of work. Basically a stinky, distracted, frustrated, hot (but lovable) mess.

I tuck him in tonight and he begins to tell me the first 39 pages of Neil DeGrasse Tyson's book *Astrophysics For People in a Hurry* (#whodoesthat), rattled off in detail all about antimatter, why teleporting cannot work right now, and came up with a possible solution (sub-particle magnets to hold your cells together). Then he went to bed, woke up an hour later thinking it was morning, came down, ate his final meal (at least it was his stomach that woke him, and not his butt) and proceeded to tell TBG all about antimatter and how the more you have, the less it weighs. With a smile and a full belly, he skipped off to bed. Yep, you're going to be just fine, kiddo. Sweet Baby Jesus, have mercy on us tomorrow.

DAY 11
March 26, 2020

There is no doubt our kids are creative problem solvers. This morning I'm greeted with a big, "Good Morning!!! Look what we did!" Damn... I love them, but that is *not* my favorite phrase to hear first thing in the morning.

I slowly turn and peek through one squinted eye and there is Lilo, with her hair in a top knot with Bianca's scrunchie. "Now she can see, Mom!" they both boast proudly, grinning from ear to ear. Well, can't knock it; they solved the problem. I'm just relieved they didn't find the clippers.

Today is meeting day at work. Only problem is, the link for a central number won't work. That turns into a thousand extra phone calls to try to pass info. (Don't be sassy and think email; that isn't working consistently either.)

TBG is head of School Command, and is taking over the teaching today because I'm trying to sort out three different issues with limited communication connectivity. However, on a bright note, our extra screens came in today, and now our kitchen table looks like Central Command. Amazingly, even with all the technology issues, the day goes relatively smoothly. and problems are being solved on the work and school front... minus a few minor injuries.

At break-time the kids go jump on the trampoline. Six minutes into a work call, I hear a bloodcurdling scream and an "I'm sorry

Bianca!" Our human puppy decided to do a fancy twisting flip and mistakenly karate chopped her in the throat. Fortunately, no crushed airway. Seriously, this is *not* the time to test Mom's nursing skills, or the hospital system's capabilities.

The Big Guy lets the kids go out to play in the afternoon, and 30 minutes later Brady comes back in crying. He fell from a tree, was scratched up a bit, but otherwise okay. Now, I need to stop here to explain a few things about our child.

First, Brady is probably one of the most adventurous little adrenaline junkies around. There's not much that scares him in regards to climbing and scaling almost anything. After catching him climbing a slick light-post, in an attempt to swing himself onto a tree to get his frisbee; calling him down from the top of downtown San Antonio's enormous playscape (I'm talking him being at the top of a 50-foot pole); and finding him numerous times at the top of the basketball hoop, we decided to put him in a Parkour class so he will at least know how to fall properly and minimize damage. Second, he cannot lie and likes to do his best to follow

rules. Third, he is as sweet as they come. Fourth, when he's emotionally overwhelmed, tired, or hungry, he cries

Okay, so he's crying and we ask what happened. The nurse in me is already assessing damage and praying to God he doesn't need medical care right now. Through the tears, he says, "I was coming down the tree, and the last branch broke and I fell on my back and I said the A-word."

"What?", trying to stifle a giggle. Apparently when he fell he responded with, "Ow, my as$!" Phew, concussion ruled out. Mommy Nurse realizes we skirted a major crisis, and explains to him that climbing is forbidden right now. Hell, breathing is risky enough.

"Unless you want Mom setting your fractured arm and using my bra as a sling, ya better settle it down."

"Okay, Mom."

Bianca is our bit more careful one. For example, her friend has a hoverboard, a motorized type of ripstick/skateboard. She gets on slowly with assistance and takes her time. Brady, on the other hand, our "Hold my beer" kid, jumps on, immediately loses his balance, and flips right on his back. (It is truly amazing this kid doesn't have brain damage yet).   Anyway, she has become pretty adept at riding it, and has decided she wants one.

"Ummmm... yeah, we're not dropping $400, kiddo. You'll have to earn it." They earn one or two tokens when they accomplish certain tasks to be able to trade in for various things. This girl doesn't miss a beat. "Okay, how many tokens, Mom?"

"Four hundred, baby girl."

"Deal."

Awesome. That should keep her positively distracted until junior high. (She's currently in third grade.)

The day is winding down relatively calmly. I'm cooking dinner, and the kids are getting a little game-time in. We try to eat pretty healthy and are always trying new meals. Bianca is our challenge, because she's a vegetarian... which really isn't the issue. The problem is, her version of vegetarian has amazingly few veggies in it.

Tonight it's a farrow bowl with roasted sweet potatoes and onion, lemon-marinated cranberries, and arugula. (Don't get all impressed...it was a Hello Fresh recipe.) I knew better than to make it like the recipe and mix it all together; they'd never eat it. So, I pretended we were fancy and made a deconstructed farrow bowl. Translation, they can't pick it apart. Now, anyone who eats arugula by itself knows how peppery it tastes. The kids give it a whirl. Brady actually likes it mixed up with sauce, and the human composter devours it. Score one for Mom.

I look over, and Bianca is actually trying all the parts. Good start, and then the face happens. The face that says I'm-eating-it-but-I'm-not-finishing-it. "Mom, something is really spicy!"

"There's nothing spicy, Bianca." (Slightly trying to psych her out).

"Yes there is, Mom!"

"The arugula might have a little peppery flavor, but that's it. You're fine, finish it up."

I had no idea that my years of high school basketball were preparing me for motherhood. My peripheral vision is awesome! I see her shove three sweet potatoes pieces in her mouth. I'm surprised, because she normally doesn't like sweet potatoes. Ahhhh... but my little clever one doesn't fail me. She nonchalantly strolls toward the bathroom.

Oh, hell no you don't.

"Get back to your seat, Bianca." There is nothing funnier than watching your kid with a mouthful of sweet potato look incredulously at you, as if she has zero idea why I'm stopping her from going to the bathroom. I wasn't born last night, child.

She's now concerned over what to do with the sweet potatoes in her mouth that she had no intention of actually chewing and swallowing.

"Come on back to your seat, Bianca, and finish eating those sweet potatoes in your mouth."

She comes slinking back in a defeated shuffle. I'm waiting for her to spit them out on the plate. She doesn't. Instead, she sloowwwllly chews and makes a face with every single chew, sipping water in between until she forces it down with only a few gagging sounds. I have to turn my back to her; the only thing I'm forcing back is hysterical laughter.

And tomorrow is Friday...

DAY 12
March 27, 2020

There are certain things that just don't cross your mind when you're in the midst of a pandemic. A dog starting a period is one of them. TBG walks in the bathroom and asks if one of the kids cut themselves, as he looks at drops of blood on the floor. Ummm... nope, but Lilo sleeps in there at night. Soooo, now what? Our other dog, Amelia, has been fixed since she was a puppy (she's almost 14). We have no idea what to do with a dog in heat (minus keeping her away from boy dogs). This might explain her weird behavior lately: not eating, acting very needy, sleeping a lot, craving sweet and salty (wait, that's me). Do I put underwear on her? I decide against it; we're so distracted, I would forget to take them off when we let her out to pee. I'm already dealing with enough messes.

Of course, this brings questions.

Brady, "Do you still get one, Mom?"

"Yes."

"How long have you had it?"

"Since I was 13."

"Does it hurt?"

"Sometimes."

"So, are you sure guys don't get a period?"

"In the physical sense, yes, I'm positive. Emotionally, I'm not so sure."

Now I have to track a dog's period... freakin' awesome.

We have school down pat today... okay, okay, TBG has it. I am head deep in meetings and getting do-outs done. I keep wondering how the hell I'm busier at home than in the office?

The kiddos rocked it out today and got all their work done. Bianca had the start of a research paper she had to turn in. There was some confusion, because Bianca wrote the whole paper on koi fish and was going to turn it in. I held it up because I didn't think she'd followed the directions correctly. TBG thought she had.

"This doesn't make sense. It says one chapter, and she's turning in a whole paper." My Type-A brain wasn't comfortable with the unknown, so I send an email to the teacher. TBG just looks at me and says, "Third Grade, not Pulitzer."

"Do it right or don't do it," I shoot back.

Two Master's prepared people aren't able to figure out a third-grade research paper... hot messes. The teacher responds and Bianca says, "Who was right?"

"Me." Bianca walks over to TBG, gives him a hug, and says, "Awww... sorry, Dad."

"Bianca, it's not a competition." I had to say that; I'm Mom. However, I was smiling just a little on the inside. Heh heh.

While TBG takes one last run to the grocery store (for a few weeks), Bianca is outside and Brady is playing video games, I take the opportunity to catch up on some work calls.

I get pretty bad allergies this time of year. I think Zyrtec should start sending me free samples with the amount I've taken over the years. When it's at its worst, I sneeze constantly, look like a plucked chicken from all the goosebumps, feel like I want to shove a back scratcher down my throat, and have had my eyes swell shut. Not an experience I would recommend putting on your bucket list.

And when I'm really lucky, everything drains at once, runs down the back of my throat, and makes me cough so hard I dry heave. I'm on a work call when the mass drainage happens. Every other sentence is me hacking, gagging, and gasping for air. I'm pretty sure the person at the other end is trying to figure out how to send me a testing kit.

I survive the meeting and go out to look for Bianca. She's at a friend's house (don't worry, they're outside... none of the parents are allowing other people's kids in their homes). They're newer to the neighborhood, and Bianca wants me to meet her friend's Mom. We meet... six feet apart. She is very nice. During our conversation she says, "I can barely keep up working from home and their homework. I feel like I'm failing at everything."

I smirk. "Far from it. Here's my cell phone number. If you have a chance, find me on FB. I have a regular post that will make you feel better." So Kim, if you're reading this... welcome to our household chaos. Pull up a chair and have a chuckle. You're doing just fine.

We made it to the weekend! Stay home, stay safe, and wash those hands.

DAY 13
March 28, 2020

First night without coughing... yay me! TBG lets me sleep in. The kids, however, decided 1030 was late enough (for the record, I never sleep that late).

"Mom! Are you awake?" they holler as they come barreling into the room.

"Do I have a choice?" I moan.

It's Saturday, our designated housekeeping day. When I went back to full-time work eight years ago, our (as in the parents') luxury was a housekeeper twice a month. The key word is "our." The kids' rooms are off-limits from services. Their rooms are their responsibility. Right now, with COVID, there is no hired housekeeping happening. We instead are using the apprentice housekeepers.

Brady comes in. "Mom, I need to use the toilet brush!" and proceeds to whip it out of its container and hold it like royalty about ready to knight someone. Did I mention I had just used it to clean the toilet in our bathroom? (This is one of the many reasons I don't keep a toilet brush in their bathroom.)

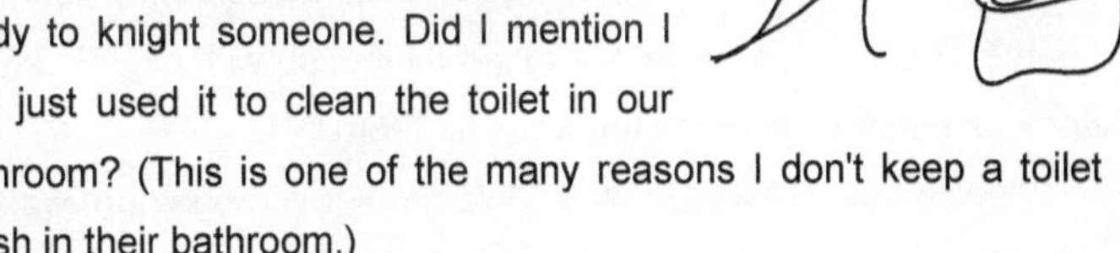

TBG comes around the corner, "Seriously, Brady... sometimes you're as thick as a whale omelet."

"What?! I didn't know Mom used it!"

"You didn't see it dripping?!"

"No."

We finish cleaning, and I look over at our shaggy Rastafarian puppy. I decide we really need to trim her up. YouTube to the rescue! We're looking for the do-it-at-home-it's-okay-if-it's-a-mess video. Instead we find every professional groomer showing us how to do it as a groomer, but nothing comes up when you put in "grooming a poodle by the unskilled-but-willing-to-give-it-a-whirl dog owner.

We sit down and watch a few anyway. TBG decides he's willing to give it a whirl. Now mind you, we only have a regular clipper. I want to watch a few more, because I didn't see one that showed how to clip the tail. And then we found one. After we get a prime shot of the clipper going right over the dog's butthole, TBG opts to put everything on hold and order an actual dog clipper. "I'm not using my clipper on the dog's a$#." So in three days Lilo will have her own clippers. (I'm still laughing at his ah-ha moment.)

I decide the dog still needs a good bath. Bianca and I get her in the tub. Bianca insists she has to get IN the tub with Lilo. "I can get her legs better if I'm in the tub with her, Mom."

"Of course, kiddo. Go for it." We get her scrubbed up, washed off, dried off, and blow-dried. A full spa day. Blow-drying is not her favorite thing. She somehow manages to stay at the maximum length of the blow dryer cord, and I look like ElastiGirl, trying to drag a 60 pound wet, collarless dog toward me to dry her. When I finally release her, she flies around the house at 900 miles an hour. Well, that'll dry the rest of her off.

The boys got the part needed to finish modifying the Nerf gun, and spent the afternoon watching YouTube, trying it out, occasionally swearing (the older one) and grinning when something worked. If you have never tried to work on a project with a very excited ADHD kid, it's quite the experience. There's usually a lot of "No wait!", "Careful, No, don't touch that!" Fortunately, no one was injured in the modifications, so we'll count it as a success.

They give her a test run and I'm not totally sure who's more excited, TBG or Brady. Keep in mind, they tried this with a single battery. The finished product will have two batteries and be twice as fast. Not so sure this will be one of our smartest moves. I think I need to have the neighborhood kids fill out a liability form before they come over and play.

We get ready to have dinner, and I mention there's a new movie on we could watch. Bianca immediately bursts into tears. Huh? My mind goes into panic mode, thinking we're cusping the teen years way too soon. My inside voice hollers, *Eight is way too young for hormone swings! Isn't it?* I'm sticking with yes.

"Baby girl, why are you crying?"

"Mom, I wanted to play a game of Life all week, and you said we could this weekend when we had more time."

"You're right, Bianca. We did say that. Okay, one game of Life coming up!"

We play by a few modified rules. First one to reach the finish line means game over. It saves a little bit of our already stretched sanity. An hour later, Bianca has two kids, is making 30K a year, and totals out around 100K in total assets. Brady ends up a single millionaire and kicks our butts.

School has done a reevaluation and decided, based on feedback, that the load might be too heavy for remote learning. Did someone send them my posts? Ummmm, it might be too heavy for the *parents* aiding with remote learning. They should have sent out a questionnaire we could fill out, anonymously asking what the various coping skills are that parents are using to stay sane. That would have been much more accurate data. No matter; thank you, teachers, for having mercy on our non-teacher souls. We will never try to compete in that category. We bow to you.

DAY 14
March 29, 2020

It's a pretty chill day for the most part. TBG put together a treasure hunt for the kids. He brings me around to do it first, and I think some of this might be above their heads. My History/English Lit-degreed husband is using Shakespeare quotes as hints. Well... I'm wrong. They pretty much blow through it, and are all excited to get their prize. I decide I probably need to brush up on my Art and Literature knowledge.

We decide to get out of the house and go for a little hour ride... just a drive in the country. We get home and our doggy clippers and brush have been delivered, but we opt to not go for it *quite* yet. We're both a teeny bit traumatized about the parts we have to shave over. The groomer is really going to hate us for this.

As TBG is starting dinner, I suggest to Brady that he sit down and LOOK OVER (that's it) his schedule to get an idea of what the week is going to bring. This is met with an immediate trembling lip and tears.

"Brady, I just said look it over, not start assignments." Interior voice: *What the hell is this child going to do in college?* Yes, yes... I've gotten a little ahead of myself.

"It's Sunday, I just want to relax!" (through tears).

"Ummm... what has the last 10 hours been?"

Brady gives me the puppy-dog teary-eyed look.

"Child, if you cannot get a little proactive in your education, you can forget college!" (Yep, it slipped out.)

"But I'm only 12, Mom!"

I'm feeling about 20% bad for my statement. "I gotcha, kiddo, but if I didn't say a word about your schoolwork, would you have looked at it tonight?"

"No." (Puppy dog eyes continue.)

"And if I didn't say a thing tomorrow, would you have jumped in and started working?"

"No." (Puppy dog eyes are diminishing.)

"Riiigghhtttt... so let's dry up those tears and look this over."

Brady's puppy dog eyes are gone, tears gone. He knows the score and is moving on. Fifteen minutes later, he's upstairs practicing his clarinet and has already answered a quick question for Science. Lord give me strength.

Parent Lesson #247: Nagging *does* work. Don't let anyone tell you otherwise.

We decide to do a movie and a meal, and serve dinner in the living room while watching *Onward* (pretty good family movie). The older brother in the movie talks in medieval dialect, and gives everyone titles (Sir, Lady, etc). Brady absolutely loves it.

"Mom, what would be my name?"

"It's a toss-up between Sir Fart-A-Lot, Sir-Eat-A-Lot, and Sir-Talk-A-Lot." Both the kids burst out laughing.

Dinner tonight is another vegetarian meal with risotto and vegetables. It smells divine. I walk over and take a look at it, smirk, look at TBG and say, "She'll never eat it." TBG doesn't have a concept of deconstructing it for our simple-palate child. Here's the recipe, I make the recipe, you eat the recipe. Now granted, he does watch out for the spiciness level. Otherwise, what he cooks is whatcha get.

I tell them both no treat until you eat all your dinner. Bianca always starts out as a game player, and then we watch the decline of enthusiasm. Every. Time. Halfway through the movie I tell her the goal is for her to be done before the movie ends. She rolls her eyes

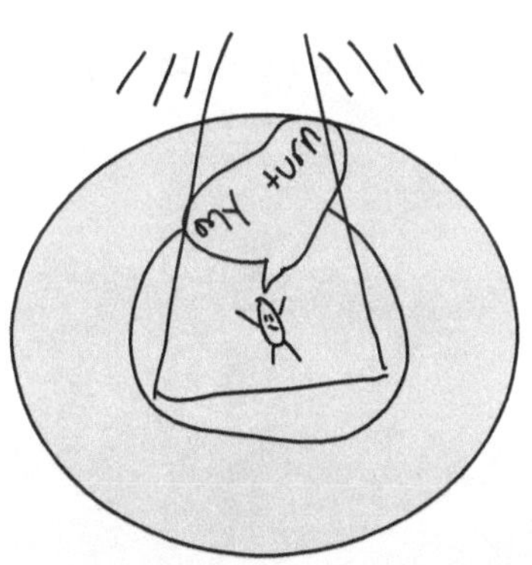

and puts one grain of risotto in her mouth. Damn, if I was a betting girl right now...

Yes, folks, the movie ends and Bianca is still at it, choking down one teeny grain of rice at a time. When reality hit that she's not getting a treat, there's a flood of tears. Sigh... life is tough, child. However, in her defense, those tears were about more than not finishing dinner. It was two weeks of pent-up anxiety over all this COVID mess. "Mommy, I hate COVID. I miss my friends and going to school. I want things back to normal."

Day 14

We do our utmost to shield them from the chaos, but when the rules suddenly change and you're told you can't hug or go near your friends... well, that's just too much for an eight-year-old to comprehend. Not looking forward to her birthday next month. I am slowly introducing the idea of a Zoom birthday party. Ugh... the things that we never imagined we would have to do!

I know this is supposed to be an upbeat story of our quarantine adventures, but sometimes reality sneaks in there. So we give hugs and snuggles, tell them they're safe and this situation is temporary (we just don't get into how long), and show them how to pull up those big girl/boy pants and keep loving life moving forward. It's the best we can do, right?

Never fear... we still have a dog clipping adventure coming up!

DAY 15
March 30, 2020

I crashed on the couch last night. I couldn't get the brain to shut off and didn't want to wake TBG. Instead I was "lulled" to sleep by one snoring dog and fighting for space by one couch-hog dog. Four glorious hours later I woke up (really wishing it was the weekend again) to the wee ones getting their morning started.

Brady, all cheery, "Mom, we're going to work out first."

"Okay, I'll work out with ya." Why not? I fell asleep in exercise pants and sports bra... and probably smell post-workout already (guarantees me my space).

These two still look like a set of grandparents working out. Bianca, all sassy and smirky, says, "Mom, can you touch your toes?" (She's doing a hurdle stretch.)

"Um, can you bend without looking like a crinkle-cut French fry?"

Day 15

Well, we get Central Command up and running. God bless those teachers. They wrote a SCHEDULE, not for the kids, but for us poor parents who couldn't find our way around Google Classroom even if wine and shots were prizes. They also eased the homework load a teeny bit. Thank you for hearing our skill-less cries... we suck... we proudly own it.

TBG is working with Bianca most of the day, and I have Brady. He was so pumped working through assignments. Praise 6.5-pound baby Jesus there are no papers due. He does have a branding assignment... as in logo branding, not ranch branding. He has to either find or come up with a quote that captures his fundamental belief. When I start helping him, he's done most of it. I'm just helping edit his presentation. I read over his quote: "It's not about what you want to be, it is about who you are."

"Wow, awesome quote, Brady. Who said that?"

"Me," he says nonchalantly.

I'm looking over at TBG and thinking to myself, *Our child, who cannot find his way out of a paper bag even if you opened one end, gave him a flashlight, and hollered for him, came up with this profound quote?*

TBG is reading my mind. "Yep, all him."

Dang, I gave birth to Socrates Jr. hidden in an awkward (but lovable) tweenie.

The kids finish up school and run out to play, but not before they receive the minimum-of-six-feet-no-matter-what-your-friend's-harebrained-idea-may-be safety speech. Thirty minutes later, Bianca comes back in crying.

"What's wrong, Bianca?"

"My friends were working on cheer routines, and needed a back spotter for their trick."

My inside voice: *Um, how do you do these tricks six feet apart? I'm not liking this story.*

Bianca continues, "I told them I've cheered before and know how to spot. They tell me they've done it professionally and don't trust me to spot."

I keep my smile and thought on the inside and think, *Ahhh little one, I have no doubt your large-and-in-charge nature brought out their little egos and the one-up game began.* Instead, I go with the PSA route. "What in God's given name were you thinking, to even consider spotting anyone?"

The girl has a comeback for everything. "Mom, I wasn't going to touch anyone."

"Well, no wonder they didn't trust you," I say jokingly. Fortunately, she gets my humor.

So being the good Mommy, I give hugs and snuggles and remind her she needs to know her truth. Bianca looks at me and says, "You can't be someone else, they've already been taken." Is this prodigy child reveal day? Am I getting punk'd?

TBG makes acorn squash soup and grilled cheese. Hoover Boy sucks it down. I'm pretty sure he has no idea what he ate. TBG gives

Bianca about two tablespoons of soup and a cheese quesadilla. FIFTEEN MINUTES later there is 1 3/4 tablespoon of soup and 3/4 of the quesadilla left. I swear I'm calling Guinness World Records. She has got to be the winner of the s.l.o.w.e.s.t eater on this planet. Fifteen more minutes and 900 redirects later, she finishes the soup and the rest of the quesadilla. Day-drinking is about ready to commence.

Let me put a public service announcement right here. It was brought to my attention by my BFF that I've made a significant number of references to alcohol throughout this book. For the record, references are for humor only, and because I know, even if you don't act on it, it crosses y'all's mind on occasion. I promise, I don't have a drinking problem. PSA done.

TBG promises Brady 45 minutes to go work on the Nerf mod. The kitchen table morphs into a Nerf laboratory. Oh, the things you'll do for your children. He's struggling to get the soldering to take it where he needs it to. Let me timeline this:

2100: Brady goes to bed (against his will). The weld is not working. but Dad isn't giving up.

2100 - 2150: TBG is now swearing because the soldering won't take, no matter what he tries. I keep my face hidden, to avoid adding fuel to the fire (but damn, it's funny.)

2200: Brady feels sick to his stomach. Really, it's more like he's so beyond excited about this gun mod. Dad lets him stay up.

2205: TBG gets the weld to hold.

2206: TBG proudly shows Brady.

2206 and 30 sec: Brady shows TBG how he connected it wrong... and he's right. (I will not come around the corner now. My life may depend on it.)

2207: More swearing from TBG. In the end, he fixes the connection and Brady has a fully modified Nerf gun. Dad is still a hero, and the world is spinning on a normal tilt again.

On a whole other note, we had to hold for the dog-clipping event. It was too wet and rainy. More to follow. Cheers to rocking out a Monday!

DAY 16
March 31, 2020

Here's a fun fact for you: poodles have hair, not fur. If you don't keep them groomed, it will just keep growing. Nope, we're still not brave enough to shave the dog. We have the clippers, have watched YouTube, and are pretty confident we're going to jack it up. We live in San Antonio; the poor gal has to be boiling in her skin. So, we really need to get over it and just go for it! I mean, what's the worst that can happen? The groomer shames us because we mowed the dog? By the time we get around to it, her hair will be long enough to be able to donate to some wig-making nonprofit.

The new school schedule is awesome. It's easy to follow for both kiddos and parents. We can actually find the assignments on Google Classroom (mostly because we keep pushing buttons and figuring it out). The workload has definitely become more evenly distributed over the week, and now they are usually done by 2-3 in the afternoon. The kids are rocking out their work and the parents have stepped back from day drinking... for now.

At lunch, we've been getting into the routine of stopping to sit and watch a nature show. Today it was on a variety of birds and fish.

The boy child of a thousand useless facts pipes up, "Did you know they can put an animal eyeball into a person, if they want one?"

Okay, I'll bite, "People have that option?"

"Well, for people losing their eyesight and for Special Tactics, they give them hawk eyes so they can see for hundreds of yards."

I'll be damned. I've been medical for 25 years, military for almost an equal amount, and never heard of that. "Huh, I'll have to check that out." The things you learn from an over-imaginative 12-year-old.

We bought a second composter, and TBG and Brady are putting it together. Somehow, Brady's version of helping translated into him climbing on top of the pergola and sweeping off the mesh.

"Brady! What in the world are you doing up there?!"

"Swinging."

"I gathered that. Remember what I told you. You break an arm, and I'll put you in a sling made out of my bra. Now get down."

"Okayyyy."

On second thought, day drinking may make a return.

As we settled down for the night, I see an email from the school district. Yep, as I anticipated. in-person school is pushed to 4 May. Meh, we've resigned ourselves to the fact they are not going back this year.

DAY 17
April 1, 2020

About five years ago, I thought it would be fun to play an April Fool's joke on the kids. They both loved to go on road trips. I told them the day before to pack their backpacks, because we were going on a surprise road trip the next day. They quickly got everything together and were ready to go by that evening. My plan was to get them into the car in the morning and then holler "April Fools!"

TBG warned me that would not be a good idea. "I think you should tell them tonight."

"But tomorrow is April Fool's Day, not today."

"Okay, but I don't say I didn't warn you."

TBG rarely tells me one of my ideas is downright stupid. So him calling me out made me question my plan. I decided to heed his advice, and when I tucked them into bed, I told them it was an April Fool's joke. They both broke down sobbing, and to this day have not let me live it down.

I didn't even bother to bring up today was April Fool's Day; 2020 has been cruel enough. Any joke played would just be irritating. Instead we found other things to amuse us.

We finally got ballsy and shaved the dog... sorta. We were too chicken to clip it close, for fear of the shave actually being noticeable. Lilo has a groomer appointment on the 22nd; we needed to take off enough to cool her, but give it enough time so the groomer won't notice.   We would have videotaped it if we'd enough hands. Here's the visual:

Both TBG and I bring her outside. We're armed with all the tricks from Youtube. What could go wrong? It's just hair, and she doesn't care. Yet, we're both a little nervous to start. A lack of coordination and skill makes for free entertainment. I decide to bite the bullet.

Before we begin, we remember we need to gently sling her back legs off the ground so she can't take off. TBG uses a dog leash to lift her hindquarters. Only one problem; he has to hold it. "Hey, make this quick, my arms will end up giving out soon."

I dive right in... which is a problem. When the fur is two inches deep and your clipper is set for 1/2 inch, it quickly bogs out the clipper. Before the dog ends up looking like the victim of a bad golfer, I turn it over to TBG. No way I can hold up those hind legs for any length of time, so I just do my best to immobilize her with my legs on either side of her hips.

He's on a damn mission! Lilo looks like she's in a rapid weight-loss program. Fur is flying everywhere! Body done! Sooo... who's doing the face?

"You want to do the face, or do you want me to keep going?" he asks.

"I'll give it a whirl." Okay... I'm ready. I reach back into the old noggin and remember from ear to nose. I got this! Awww, dang it...after my first go, Lilo now looks like a poodle with a Schnauzer nose. How in the hell do you get right by the nose without shaving it off?! The video didn't look that hard, and none of the dogs in the video tried to run back between the groomer's legs. We had Brady hold the leash for her hindquarters. Oy veh, five milliseconds later: "My arm hurts... I'm tired."

"Seriously, Brady, Lilo is trying to go in reverse here... hold the damn leash!"

I opt to just use the scissors to trim the rest. And for all those wondering...TBG has the honor of shaving her back end. He's just glad it isn't his razor.

We are on Day 3 of the kids rocking school and parents staying

mostly sane. Of course, now our oldest has confiscated my extra computer screen, because it's easier for him to work.. This comes with slight annoyance from me. My inside voice starts to ramble on. What the hell... I can't remember the last time I had anything of mine. Food... "Can I have a bite (the size of my head)?" Clothes... "Can I borrow that sweatshirt (that will end up lost)?"; sitting on the couch... "Can I sit with you?" Translation: "Can I sit nearly on you, steal your blanket, and ask you to rub my feet/back/head, and if you're eating something, have a bite of that too?"

As I'm finishing writing this, TBG goes to the liquor cabinet and takes a shot of bourbon.

"Curing coronavirus?"

"There's a reason why those old farts survived all those epidemics back in the day." Well, he has a point. I'm sure there has to be some research on that.

We're over hump day and sliding down to the weekend, where hopefully I can find a little of my own.

DAY 18
April 2, 2020

Have you ever been in a situation where it's not going in a way you were hoping at first, then it turns around, and you realize that's not quite what you wanted either? Yeah, that's what the last two weeks of the kids' online schooling has been for us.

Week One basically kicked our behinds in every way imaginable. A couple rounds with a WWE wrestler would have done less damage. The workload was heavy, the technology was new, finding information was a challenge, teleworking and managing school schedules was an ugly dance, and we were completely beat by the end of the week.

Week Two rolls in, and based on feedback from a lot of whooped parents, the schedules were adjusted and information reorganized... and POOF, like magic, things were manageable. The kids are working more independently, and were able to juggle a bit better.. .at least a ball or two stays in the air now!

Buutttt... there's another side (I can't call it a downside, more of a distracting side). They have more time to free-think, get into things, and say and do some pretty funny stuff.

The morning starts with a dance party in the kitchen. The song "I Like Big Butts" comes on. Woohoo... fun song to dance to! That is, until I started listening to the words. Funny how parenting gives you extra sense to hear Every. Single. Word. of a song that you never paid any attention to before. Halfway through, "Next song, Alexa!" (TBG just laughs when he sees my face.)

The kids get a bit of their schoolwork done and then take a little break.

"Mommy, will you come jump with me on the trampoline?" asked Bianca.

"Sure, why not?" As long as there are no attempts at fancy moves, I'm good. After 15 minutes of building my resistance to vertigo, we took a break and flopped on the trampoline.

"Mom, you should be a therapist."

Inside voice: *Hell no!* Don't get me wrong, I admire my therapist friends tremendously. I just know that's definitely not my skillset.

Outside Voice: "Why do you think that?"

"Because I can come and talk to you," (direct hit to the heart) "and you're calm." (Ummm...she obviously doesn't have a great memory.)

"Calm? What about when I get on your butt about things?"

Bianca, smirking, "Weellll, I probably deserved it." (Dang it...I really needed to record that confession!)

I laugh because I've had a few people tell me they thought I would be a good therapist, and had I never considered it? I'll be honest. I'm too much of a problem solver. I like to come up with the solution. My dream job would be to be part of a think tank, where a team goes into companies on their last legs and assists in solving the issues. I'm not sure I'd have the patience to wait an extended period of time for someone to have their "ah ha" moment. Supporting friends, sure, definitely not a problem. Providing professional guidance, not so much. It would probably go something like this.

Session #40

"Okay, Mr. Jones, let's talk about how the week went. You were working at identifying what triggers your anger."

"Yes, and I still can't figure it out. I was irritable most of the afternoon."

"Well, did anything happen?"

"My mom called at noon."

"And?"

"And nothing... she called and needed a little money again. But that's nothing new."

"Dude, we've been having this discussion for 6 months. Hello, your Mom is triggering you! C'mon!"

And that would probably be the end of my therapist days.

After lunch it starts to rain, and Bianca was nowhere to be seen. "Where's Bianca?" I asked, looking around.

TBG grins. "Jumping on the trampoline."

"It's raining out."

"Doesn't seem to be bothering her."

And there she is, happy as a clam, jumping in the rain. I probably should join her. The youth have it right.

Brady finished all his schoolwork, and before you know it, out comes the modified assault Nerf gun. I am not sure TBG was wise in this decision.

"Brady, don't even think of it."

"What?!"

"Don't think of shooting me!" I holler, as I swipe the Nerf gun from him. "Game on!"

"Mom! No fair, you can't do that!"

"Oh yes I can. I'm Mom. Muhahahahahaha... better run!"

Thirty minutes later he's pelted with Nerf bullets. The couple of yelps tell me they stung a bit. Before he can gain any advantage, I end the game, using the excuse that I have to get dinner started. (Not sure I really get any advantage here... dinner or pelted with a semi-automatic Nerf).

Before dinner, Bianca decides to do an opera ballad. It reminds me how frustrating all this COVID drama is, and how it's foiled yet another plan.

"Girl, we are getting your butt into the theater when this is all over."

Bianca just gives me a sassy look and continues the made-up ballad. Much like an Italian operetta, I have no idea what she is saying. The child lives in her own world.

About three seconds after dinner ends, Bianca pipes up, "Can I have a treat?"

"There's a ton of fruit in the fridge."

"That's not a treat!"

"Um, your treat is every meal you get, child."

She cautiously gives me an eye-roll... slowly pulls out applesauce... still thinking. She is wisely keeping any comments to herself.

DAY 19
April 3, 2020

It's a serious "cats on crack" kind of day. The kids finish school by noon and drive us bonkers the rest of the day. All this rain is not helping our cause. Lord help us if it rains more than it's sunny during this crisis.

I have zero idea how we end up talking to the kids about Lilo in heat, but hell's bells, we do. Bianca starts, "Well, it's good she has her period; at least we know she isn't having puppies right now."

"When they have their period that means they're fertile and could get pregnant," I explain.

Brady chimes in, "They have periods twice a year, and they give off a scent that says, 'Hey boys, over here, I'm ready to mate.' And then they act really loopy."

It takes every bit of my power not to burst out laughing. Where do they come up with this stuff!?

TBG has been doing the majority of the cooking. Not sure exactly what he's been feeding them, but WOOF it catches up with both of them today. It nearly kills TBG and me. This isn't a little toot; this is trucker-level-melt-your-face-off flatulence, like I've never smelled before. TBG and I just look at each other incredulously.

TBG, trying to speak without taking a breath or opening his mouth, mumbles, "What in the world did they eat!?!"

"Umm, the bean burrito you made Brady?!" I reminded him.

"Bianca didn't eat that! What's her excuse?"

"Now that I think of it, maybe there were too many greens in the smoothie today."

"OMG, back off the healthy stuff. It's going to kill our sense of smell, and we'll think we all have COVID."

The kids decide they want to watch a movie "series" and pick the Minions. (Yes, we know you're smiling, Johneda O'Connor. It's a favorite of our friend.) This is not a great idea for kids who are already wired for sound. By the time the movie is over and they're heading to bed Bianca, decides she's going to imitate the sumo wrestler minion and proceeds to give herself a wedgie and run around the house... then, turn around and help her brother do the same, while both are yelling "Giddy-up," racing around the house. Note to self: only *Sound of Music* type movies in the evening.

We're chalking this insanity up to a long (although a bit more relaxed) week. It's Friday, folks. We continue to embrace the zany, laugh at the silly, and give lots of hugs.

DAY 20
April 4, 2020

OMG! The rain will not stop! More rain = kids with more energy. I was greeted with kids in rare form this morning. Up the stairs, down the stairs, diving on the couch, around the kitchen. They obviously had a good night's sleep. No worries, we have creative ways of expending that energy. Housework! Muhahahaha...

There's an upside and a downside to having the kids complete housework. Upside, they're learning responsibility and the importance of helping out the family. The downside: "clean" is a subjective word. Growing up, if we didn't clean to Mom's specifications, she cleaned behind us. Naturally, when we figured this out, we got worse at housekeeping.

It's one of the "kid secrets" I kept tucked in the back of my noggin for the future. And here we are. So, I try to educate and have them come back when their "cleaning" looks more like a tornado came through, in hopes they'll realize doing it right the first time is the fastest route.

"Bianca, come on back and let's look at the mirrors. When you wash them you should be able to see your reflection, not a foggy image of yourself."

"Brady, thank you for cleaning the litter box. Now can you clean the 30 pounds of litter that dropped on the floor?"

Day 20

"It's great you swept, but it's more helpful if you come back and sweep up and throw away the piles you collected."

Sometimes it is so tempting to just do it myself, but no, dammit, we're committed to raising independent, relatively neat, kids. But phew, it is exhausting.

Okay, it wasn't all slave labor today. Bianca "helped" me bake... another independent task we're working on. In reality, it was more like the taste tester in every phase of the recipe. Brady helped TBG modify another Nerf gun. I swear we're going to have an arsenal of automatic Nerfs by the time this pandemic is over. I have zero idea where this fits into raising the independent child, but hell, they may come in handy with all this chaos going on.

All this home time is leaving TBG too much free time on his hands. A few years back his car died, and we agreed, since he drives cars forever, he should get the car he wants. The result was a 2008 BMW M3... a grown man's Barbie Doll. His goal was to be able to modify it to his liking. It's been an ongoing love affair. He is now modifying his car lights so they shine "angel eyes". I have no idea what that means, but in another month we may have a new rendition of the Batmobile. Pretty sure he needs an intervention soon.

Being home more, I'm trying to be creative so the kids aren't falling into complacency. Tonight, I thought I'd surprise the kids with homemade Wendy's Frosties for dessert after dinner.

"Mom, what's that?" they both chime in as I'm serving the Frosties in the bowls.

"Dessert!"

"That is so cool! It looks like dog poop!"

"Okay, yes, but it will be the best-tasting dog-poop-looking-dessert you have ever tasted."

And it was.

Lord have mercy on my soul, tomorrow they are calling for more rain. I should be peeling them off the walls by mid-morning. Does anyone need a house cleaned?

Day 20

DAY 21
April 5, 2020

Lordy was the weekend long. I'm honestly glad school starts back up tomorrow to channel that damned energy. Woof! Today was "kids say and do the damndest things" day.

We're starting the morning with something that vaguely resembles Folk Dancing. Out of the blue, the kids holler, "Alexa, play bagpipe music!" Say what?! When in the world did they get into bagpipe music? An instant later, there's Frick and Frack attempting their rendition of Riverdance. I nearly die of laughter. Bianca is attempting to be very straight-faced, looking like she's concentrating on getting all the steps (of a dance she doesn't know) right.

Then there's Brady. I'm not even sure how to describe it in a way to give you the hilarious vision that was unfolding behind his sister. Picture a cross of folk dancing with Gumby legs. Here's this kid bobbing up and down and randomly kicking his legs around. He then decides to add in the air bagpipes and make faces while he is "playing." At that point, I just bust out laughing.

I do what any strategic parent would do. I record it, and it will be used for bribery material with future boy- and girlfriends.

While they goof off, TBG decides he wants to try a bread recipe. He made a comment about using yeast. The kids are apparently not only fluid in funky folk dancing, but yeast varieties. Bianca decides to educate Dad. "Did you know there are two kinds of yeast? The kind you make bread with and the kind girls have." (Scrunching up her nose).

Neither of us knows what to say. So we don't.

Brady doesn't miss a beat. "Yeah, I don't think the girl stuff is good."

TBG and I just sit there, in awe, trying not to laugh. We think it's better left alone.

TBG gave it a go with the baking yeast (just to make sure we're all clear here). and his bread flopped. Okay, it wasn't a complete flop. It was just super-dense. The garbage disposal wolfed it down.

Okay, as all parental units know, kids tend to be messy, but boys seem to be able to take it to a whole other level that both disgusts and amazes me at the same time. Brady is sitting at the table eating rice by shoveling it into a mouth that is literally placed at the very edge of the plate, wide open, attempting to receive the food, yet still dropping it on the floor.

TBG was simultaneously in awe and annoyed. "How are you missing your mouth!? It's all over the floor."

I am equally in awe and annoyed. "I think you eating dinner is the Eighth Wonder of the World."

Brady, way too focused on killing his hunger pains: "Huh? What? I'm just eating."

I sigh, as I come to a possible realization. "Pretty sure you won't be the one to give me grandchildren."

Brady excuses himself from the table, walks into the living room, and with great grandeur, loudly passes gas. Smiles. "Ahhh, better." He then comes back to the table and continues to shovel the remaining food on his plate.

"Yep, definitely no grandchildren."

DAYS 22-23
April 6 & 7, 2020

The most exciting part of the last two days has been hearing about TBG's grocery adventure, ordering post-surgical PJs (Lilo) and glowsticks (kids) and helping the kids make special birthday videos for Oma and Uncle Ben.

I can't seem to shake the sniffly, nose-runny, hacking remnants of the flu I had a couple weeks ago. With my luck it's probably a mild case of COVID, but I'll never know; it's nearly impossible to get tested right now. So, to avoid either catching or giving something, TBG has been kind and going out to do the grocery runs. You know your life has hit a new level when the topic of the day is if you were able to get toilet paper during your grocery run.

"Hey babe, how was the store?"

"Bare. No toilet paper, paper towels, disinfecting cleaning products, and now no meat."

"No meat?!"

"Yep, and whatever was there has already doubled in price."

"Well, good thing we just went to Costco before this all hit."

"Yep, but if it stays this way, we might be buying items on the black market."

He was joking, but at the same time there was probably a little truth in it. I can only imagine what my grandchildren's history lessons will encompass.

"Now, who can tell me what items stores were running out of, and why? Korona?"

"They were running out of toilet paper, paper towels, and Lysol spray because, well, I don't know... I guess because they were going to be stuck in their house, eating more and would need to poop more. So, they needed more toilet paper to wipe their butts and paper towels and Lysol spray to clean the toilet."

"Very good, Korona."

I mentioned earlier, Lilo, our standard poodle, has started her period. Fortunately, we were on the ball and already had her appointment to get her fixed booked. She's the sweetest dog, but like all puppies, a hot mess. I was not looking forward to a 60-pound puppy with limited coordination running around the house with a cone on. Then, I remembered seeing the surgical pajamas. Bingo! Exactly what we need. TBG thought I was crazy.

"You're ordering what?"

"Post-surgical PJs for Lilo."

"They make those for dogs?!"

"Yep, they do."

"I think I've seen everything now."

"Hey, it's better than having her, in all her uncoordinated-ness, walk around with a big ol' cone."

"True... if it's not complicated to get her into the PJs "

"Meh, we'll figure it out."

One of the challenges in our newly quarantined lifestyle has been keeping the kiddos entertained when they're not occupied with school. We were all watching YouTube videos and saw kids doing the "glowlight dance". This is where they dance in the dark with what looked like glow sticks attached to their clothes. After a little research, we found out it was strings of LED lights attached to their clothing. Seemed like inexpensive entertainment. Let's add it to the Amazon order. Since the pandemic, I'm pretty sure Amazon has their own driver for our house.

On the upside, COVID has stretched the kids' self-entertainment. The latest is singing customized birthday songs for family and friends, and I post them on Facebook. Last night it was an opera rendition of Happy Birthday for Oma. Tonight it is a *Star Trek* version for Uncle Ben. They may have a shot on Broadway.

DAY 24
April 8, 2020

It's the Bianca Show-and-Tell today.

First thing in the morning, Bianca is grunting, sighing, mumbling under her breath, flopping around on the couch in the family room. There's no way you can't hear her, but I'm not acknowledging her maladapted request for help.

"Mommmm, I needed help!"

I walk over. "Ahhh, that was a lot better than all the fussing around you were doing."

Bianca, now mad, slumps down on the couch. "I don't need your help anymore."

"Okay," and I about-face back to my computer.

Ten minutes later… "Mom, could you help me, please?"

"Of course! Glad you asked!" (Inside voice: *Mom 1, Little Miss 0.*)

I continuously repeat the words my friend Heidi told me, "Break her will a little, not her spirit." Or was that the other way around? Either way, teach the lesson, don't crush her. The statement makes complete sense. How to go about it is the question I haven't quite been able to answer.

Dinner time is my least favorite time of the day. Bianca has been a vegetarian since age 5. No kidding. She just looked at me one day and said, "Mommy, I am a vegetarian."

"Do you know what 'vegetarian' means, baby?"

Day 24

"Yes, I don't like to eat meat."

And that was that. I would be a bit more pleased if she would eat vegetarian food besides pasta, cheese, and cucumbers. Nonetheless, we're always introducing new foods. Tonight it's vegetarian meatballs, and Bianca asked to serve dinner. My hope is she buys into eating it, since she's serving it.

"Mom, here is yours!" She proudly presents me with four meatballs on the plate. "And here is mine!" One poor little lonely meatball on her plate.

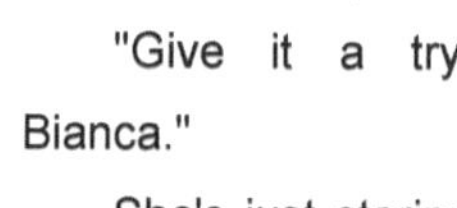

"Give it a try, Bianca."

She's just staring at it, probably hoping it will turn into a Cadbury egg. She takes four sips of her drink and starts a lot of idle chatter, takes a bite, mentally analyzes each chew... smiles... and says she likes it.

Hoping to keep the positive vibes going strong. "Awesome!" (Inside voice: *Wait for it.*) As right as rain, this child proceeded to establish a Guinness World Record for the longest time to eat a single vegetarian meatball.

"Girl, finish."

"I am!"

Ten minutes later... no joke. "Bianca, if you say you like it, why has it taken you longer to finish half of that poor, lonely meatball than it has for Brady to finish two full meatball subs?"

Bianca, exasperated, "I am eating it!"

Two minutes later...

Using my warped sense of humor to diffuse my exasperation, "Sooooo, are you savoring it?"

Bianca bursts into tears. "I don't like it!"

As I'm hugging her, TBG sarcastically comes back with, "And the Mom of the Year Award goes to..."

My inside voice: *Sweet Baby Jesus, give me strength.*

Bedtime is always an adventure. This is another area where she could be a record winner: the ability to drag out bedtime. She's worked on mastering this art since she was a baby. Unlike Brady, whose routine consisted of bath, change diaper, give bottle (warm or cold, didn't matter), lay in crib, give kiss, and leave room, Bianca's was much more complex. It started the same: bath, change diaper, and then got complicated....rock in the rocking chair, bottle at 88.6453765 degrees, sing song, and had to be more than 3/4 asleep before you laid her down.

Tonight I get her up to her room at 8:15 to read with me, figuring a good 20 minutes will settle her down. W.R.O.N.G., wrong, wrong. Instead it's a bombardment of questions and comments over 2.5 minutes while she flops around the bed:

"Mommy, how many days until my birthday?"

"Mommy, how many days until Easter?"

"I hope the Easter Bunny makes it."

(Me too.)

"Mommy, did you ever do funny things as a kid, like Daddy?"

(He, by far, beat me.)

"Mommy, we need to cook treats for the Easter Bunny."

"Mommy, we need to put the treats for him in the plastic eggs he left last year."

"Mommy, can you tell me a story."

"Mommy, will you rub my back."

(Ding ding ding... finally losing steam)

"Mommy, I'm so excited that the Easter Bunny is coming. I'm going to decorate eggs and make things for him because he'll be tired."

(So is your Mommy.)

Thirty minutes later, eyes start to close and Mom gets a few minutes of peace.. .until we start again tomorrow.

Cheers to all the parents holding it together, even when they want to fall apart. We got this!

DAY 25
April 9, 2020

I think the kids are starting to get a little cray-cray. We give them large brown paper to design Easter Eggs to post on our garage door. They're both excited and decide they're going to help each other out with their designs. Sigh...

Let's clarify what "help" sounded like between siblings.

"I'll write on your egg, Bianca."

"Okay! Just put it right here in this color."

"No, I don't want to do that!"

And here we go; an argument ensues. Now reverse roles, and yep, same control issues, same argument.

"Brady, can I put a decoration on yours?"

"Okay! Use the red one and put a dot right here. No, no Bianca, not there, over here!"

"But I want to put it here!"

TBG, looking at both of them, says, "Are you freaking kidding me?! You agree to put a design on each other's Easter Egg, but are mad at each other when you do it!?!"

Brady and Bianca both look at Dad with big blank stares.

And that's how most of the day goes. Both of them come up with some harebrained idea, think it's the greatest thing ever, and then dissolve into an argument when the other one doesn't follow it to a T.

By the end of the day TBG and I are wiped out.

"They were a pair of boobs today," TBG says as he flops on the couch.

"Yes they were," I respond as I flop on the other end of the couch. We're not big drinkers. However, the porter we split goes down really easy tonight.

DAY 26
April 10, 2020

Working at home has its upsides and downsides. A major downside is that I often have no idea what day it is. I show up for meetings because my Outlook calendar tells me to. Today was a school holiday. I had zero idea if I was supposed to be working... so I did just in case. The only thing I was absolutely sure of was that it was a day of the week that ended in "y." #losinggriponreality

We have to take Lilo to the veterinarian at 0730 this morning for her surgery. This is the first time I've been out of my house in three weeks. I'm beyond excited, and find it to be way more anticlimactic than I was hoping. I'm over here with the *Sound of Music* playing in my head, ready to burst out to see the world. Instead, it's a five-minute drive with a puppy that has car anxiety and drools like a St. Bernard; a five-minute wait in our car while they do a COVID19 background check; and then a quick drop and go. So underwhelming... bummer.

We get home, and TBG is all over it. He gives the Mini-Mes a little project to keep them occupied for an hour or so. He has coins and bills from various countries, and gives the currency to them to organize in a book. When they're done, they come over to show me their work.

Bianca, all proud, showing me a Taiwanese bill: "Mom, the guy on the bill is Stewart Bob."

"The general on that bill is Stewart Bob?"

"Yes, I named him after Stewart and Bob on the Minions."

"Ahhhh... I'm sure he's loving his new name."

TBG and I both had projects to work on, so we told the kids they needed to play together quietly for a little while. Parenting Rule #35: never quantify "a little while"; it will never be as long as you want. Amazingly, they self-entertained long enough for me to wonder if they were plotting to overthrow the establishment... but it still wasn't enough to really care. The next thing I know, I hear TBG: "Kids, come down and pick up your stuff on the table."

WHAT. IS. HE. DOING?!

Did he overlook Parenting Rule One-oh-#$%^-one.... NEVER bother children who are happily and quietly playing with each other? I look up in horror as I hear the mini-stampede come barreling down the stairs, and hang my head.

Both in unison, "Can I have my Pez candy?"

My standard answer anytime candy comes into question is, "You need to eat lunch."

Bianca crams a banana in her mouth. "Now can I?"

"No, that's not lunch."

Brady, staring at the open refrigerator, "I'm hungry."

"When are you not?"

ONE HOUR later, two kids fed, kitchen table picked up and back upstairs playing. As we're settling back into our projects, I look over at my Beloved. "What in God's name were you thinking?"

"What?"(Sheepish smile.) "They needed to pick up."

"You have seriously lost it. Who in God's name disrupts two kids playing together QUIETLY!"

We went and picked up Lilo from the vet's at 4:30. Poor dog looked like Bob Marley let her sample one too many blunts. TBG loads her gently into the car. I was a little concerned because she's stoned and won't sit down. I figured we were five minutes from home and she'd be fine. Little did I know sitting was the least of our issues.

About one minute into the five-minute drive, I look back and see she's still standing. Just as I turn back around, all of a sudden hear a faucet running.

TBG's eyes get big. "Is she peeing?"

"I don't know. All I can see is a stone-black pile of curls blankly looking back at me."

Thirty seconds later, the odor creeps to the front and wraps around my nose hairs.   "Yep, pretty sure that was pee." I look back again and she's out of sight. "And now she's lying in it."

When we get home, we decide we'll deal with the port-a-john in the back later. I want to clean her up and put her into her post-surgical pajamas I bought-on Amazon. Anything to avoid needing a cone. The poor dog is klutzy enough without something wrapped around her head. Four tries later, we get her dressed. The first three times we stuck it on backwards. The stoned dog became amazingly more inflexible with every attempt. We finally get it on and she now looks like she should be on a Jane Fonda workout video. Fortunately, it does not seem to be bothering her.

When we finally get everyone settled down and into bed this evening, Bianca decides she has questions. Shocking... not. My children are going to solve all the world's problems between the hours of 8 and 9 pm.

"Mommy when I grow up, you won't be able to give me kisses and say goodnight every night because I'll live on my own."

"Well, you could call me at night."

"Well, I *will* call, and you'll probably be eating pizza and drinking beer."

"Does that even sound like Mom?" Where in the world does she come up with this stuff?!

"Well, you'll be old then and probably be going through a midlife crisis."

"Probably."

DAY 27
April 11, 2020

To say Bianca is excited for Easter is an understatement.

TBG and I started preparing the kids a couple weeks ago by telling them the Easter Bunny might not be able to make it with everything going on. We thought we were going to get a little party-planning reprieve. Not. So. Fast. Randolph Elementary sends out a letter they received from Easter Bunny HQ; the WHO cleared him for delivery.

Now, parents, we've just entered a Y-in-the-road moment. Do we continue to water the seeds we planted earlier on, OR do we share this information? No judgment... I know y'all would pause for a second too.

Good parents win over lazy parents, and we read them the letter. However, we tell them that due to shortages, he may have to modify his drop-off. Brady does the skeptical "Oh, okay." Bianca's eyes look like she just won the lottery, complete with a high-pitched squeal (I should be tone-deaf by next year).

This is the rest of the week:

Monday: "Mom, are you excited for Easter?"

"Not as much as you are, Bianca."

Tuesday: "Mom, I'm excited for Easter. We can bake mini-cakes and put them in little plastic Easter Eggs we collected from him last year."

"Ummm... why?"

"Because then he has treats to find."

"Pretty sure he's not going to have much time for that. Remember, he still has to take precautions."

"Oh yeah."

Wednesday: "Mommy, are you excited for Easter? I am so excited, I wish it was here already."

"So I noticed."

Thursday: "Mommy, how many days until Easter?"

I have to find a calendar because I've really lost track of the days. "Three."

"OMG, I can't wait!"

Friday: "Mommy, Easter is almost here. Should we bake him something?"

My inside voice hollers, *I really do not want to bake!* But my outside Mommy voice prevails. "Well, he doesn't have a lot of time and may not have room to carry it. I think carrots are fine."

Saturday morning: Bianca bouncing on our bed to wake me up. "It's almost Easter!"

I am racking an eye open to see a wildly excited little girl and an equally excited 57-pound poodle in my face.

"Mommy, why did we fix Lilo if we don't have a boy dog?"

Yay, a topic besides Easter. "Because if she gets around boy dogs when she's in heat, she could get pregnant."

Bianca doesn't miss a beat. "That's when the boy dog gets on the back of her and goes like this." (Thrusting her hips)

I now want to go back to the Easter discussion. "Yes, that's how they mate." It is way, way, way too early for this conversation.

Bianca, now giggling, "That's how dogs do it. People don't do that. The boy just puts the sperm in the girl and they have a baby."

Where does she get this stuff!? As a prior labor and delivery nurse, I have no problem openly discussing the topic with my kids. It's just way too early in the morning for this discussion. "Why don't you go get dressed so we can start the day?"

Saturday evening, we decide to have a little movie night. We watch the new Trolls movie. "Holy crap, it's $20 to rent! Dang, that's a lot."

TBG, always the more rational one: "Well considering

we pay $24 when we go, just for the movie, then $80 for food and then they con us into a bazillion bucks for arcade games after... meh, this is cheap."

"Hmmm...good point. Movie it is!"

Ten minutes into the movie, Brady hears something at the door. He looks and finds a few goodies from our neighbor Kimberly and her kiddos... including a bottle of wine, brownies, and a craft for Bianca. We started Skype crafts with our girls. It keeps them socialized, mentally stimulated and productive, and gives the Moms a few precious minutes of sanity. Did I mention I love my neighbor?

I barely make it through the movie without falling asleep. We started it at six, and no, I didn't have any of the wine. After we finish, Bianca wants to watch an Easter show, because that's what you do on Easter Eve. Yep, you guessed it. I crash and am woken up by TBG at 11.

"Did the Easter Bunny come yet?"

"Nope, she was asleep on the job. But the kids got the carrots ready for her. Go read what they wrote on the paper plate."

They each wrote a little message to the Easter Bunny. Bianca's said "Have a great night. I love u!" Brady's said, "Have a fun and safe trip." Too cute.

"Dang lazy bunny."

The stash was a little smaller than normal, but who cares; they were pumped just knowing there was something to look forward to tomorrow. The Easter Bunny made sure to hide them really well... fewer to find, but harder to find. Muhahaha.. .work for it, kids!

DAY 28
April 12, 2020

The child who was so "whatever" about the Easter Bunny coming is awake at 4 am and proceeds to wake up his little sister. Of course, the only natural thing to do next is to wake up Mom and Dad. Baaddddd choice.

Both heathens: "Mom, Dad... wake up... it's Easter."

"What time is it?" I moan.

TBG is not amused. "Kids, it's 4:30 in the morning! Go back to bed."

Yeah, that doesn't happen.

We have repeat performances at 0530, 0630 and 0730, each time met with some version of "Are you two nuts?!" At 0730, we finally drag our sorry parent butts out of the warm, comfortable bed, get dressed, and slide onto the couch while two kids, already jonesing on candy (c'mon, we weren't born yesterday) speed around the house and yard, searching for more goods to keep their high going strong.

Well, no point in a healthy breakfast; they've had enough calories to fuel a rocket ship. Since the glow lights came in, the kids decide they have to work on their dance routine. That should burn off some of that sugar high.

Brady hollers, "Alexa, play *Sandstorm* by Darude." That boy has an internal volume control issue.

Pause here for a minute. I love music, but never ever know the name of the darn song or the artist. I just like the beat most of the time. "Hmmm, I never heard that song before."

TBG smirking. "Oh yes you have... just listen."

In an instant, I'm transported back to my clubbing days in Germany, at A8, watching our new flight nurse, Alison, rave-dancing with glow sticks. (And now she's the commander of our old medevac unit, and we're all jealous.) Brian and I proceed to show our Mini-Mes the proper way to dance to club music. We can't figure out if their expression is awe or horror. I'm going with awe.

The kids spend a good part of the day choreographing their dance. I will say they're pretty creative.

Brian takes advantage of the time and puts his new lights in the car. "Come check it out."

I can't help but smirk. His obsession is humorous. "Are these the lights that wink at you or something like that?"

"Never mind, smart-ass."

"Awwww..."

He gets over it and shows them to me later that evening... and I still have no idea what looks different. But hey, he's happy.

We get a surprise at our doorstep from a dear friend. Easter baskets for all, and a bottle of red wine for Mommy. Score! Kids stay high, Mommy stays mellow. Two bottles of wine in two days... my posts may be sending the wrong (or right) message.

We decide, after a chill day and family dinner, to end the day with a nice family walk. One-quarter of a mile into a two-mile walk we come upon a fledgling bird on the sidewalk. I put it in low bushes about six inches where it was, so the Mommy bird could find her baby. The next 1-3/4 miles is a cross between Bianca pleading, begging, and defending a case for going back and getting the baby bird.

TBG thinks his explanation will resolve the issue. "Bianca, nature has a way of taking care of their own."

I just shake my head. We've owned this model for nine years, and yet he still misses the mark. "Not comforting, dude."

Bianca, through tears: "THE BABY BIRD IS GOING TO DIE WITHOUT HIS MOMMY!"

I look over at TBG. "Told ya."

TBG just rolls his eyes when she's not looking. Nine-year-old girls are very much a mystery to him.

I tell Bianca when we get home that she can research how to care for baby birds and we can check on the bird tomorrow. If the bird is there and her research tells us how, we will get the bird. This is not the answer she was looking for. More crying and pleading ensued.

I gave TBG a warning. "Be prepared, we may be owning a bird tomorrow."

TBG is not having it. "Like hell. When we go walk the dogs tomorrow morning, that bird is going to miraculously fly away... dead or alive."

"You're as dramatic as her."

When we get home, I tell Bianca I'll help her research. "For all we know, Bianca, it might be more harmful to move him."

"BUT MOMMY, I DON'T WANT A COYOTE TO EAT HIS GUTS OUT!" Lots more tears; ugh, she knows how to tug on those heartstrings! Theater awaits you, child.

I pull up a Google search on fledgling birds. "Look, Bianca, a fledgling may look like it fell out of the nest, but probably was kicked out in order to learn how to fly. So, the best thing is to put him in a safe place in the shade... which we did!"

That is obviously not the right answer. The right answer is, she wants to give it a try for a day, and if caring for the bird doesn't work, we will then listen to Google. Ummm... yeah... no go.

Don't worry, we're already prepared for an early morning wake-up to go find a baby bird.

Hope your Monday starts out way less dramatic than ours.

DAY 29
April 13, 2020

I have no idea how we skirted this, but Bianca doesn't say one word about the bird this morning. And like any intelligent parents, we didn't say a peep. Sometimes karma is kind.

The kids have the day off, so we aren't completely lucky. Keeping them entertained is sometimes harder to manage than teleworking and homeschooling. It is absolutely amazing that when they have the WHOLE DAY FREE, they cannot figure anything to do. Yet when it's time for bed, the kids decide it is time to learn a new language, take up calligraphy, write a novel, or build a time-travel machine.

Just as TBG and I start getting into our projects, young Brady decides it's time for some Dad-son time. "Dad, wanna come play Tetris?"

"Can't right now, buddy, we're on the clock."

Bianca dramatically flops down next to me.

"Last night you wanted to write, read, and draw. Why don't you do that now?" She just shoulder-shrugs and sighs. I'd normally be more annoyed, but I'm just grateful she didn't bring up the bird.

When they do figure out what to do, it's something that involves destroying half the house. Bianca looks at me with big ol' puppy eyes. "Mom, can we build a fort? Pleeaassse!"

Damn her. "Okay, but upstairs in the loft." They have their friend down the street on Skype "building" with them. Noisy!

An hour later it looks like we have a shantytown in our loft...complete with a library and escape tube. How funny—they were so gung-ho when they were building it, but gung-no when it was time for clean-up. "Hey guys, if you're done, please pick it up."

"Awwww Mom, can you help us?"

"Have you both gone and lost your mind? I didn't make this mess, and you promised me you would clean this up."

"But there is so much stuff here!"

"Maybe you should have thought of that before you pulled every blanket and cushion upstairs. Happy cleaning! I know you'll do great!" (All about that positive parenting!)

We do our best to keep the outside chaos of the world outside. Besides, we have plenty of chaos IN the house, why do we need to add to it? We do not watch the news (FB posts it anyway), and we try to limit our discussion of world messes to when the kids are not around. It's not that we don't want them to be aware; we do, but we want to filter it. We don't want them to waste energy on issues they have zero control over. We keep a schedule, keep positive attitudes, make hygiene a priority, and teach them the importance of being prepared versus panicking. I decide we should order some face masks now, and give them time to come in.

Now, I know what some of you are thinking: why don't I sew my own? Well, let me tell you, I am from a family of very craft-talented folks and amazingly, I was not blessed with that gene.

TBG didn't believe how talentless I was until he saw me sew up my flight suit years ago. It was hot out, and my flight suit stuck to my leg when I bent down, and it ripped right up the seam of my backside. I brought the torn flight suit over to his house, in hopes he would help a girl out.

"You can't sew that yourself?"

"You seriously do not know how bad I suck at sewing. I can sew buttons only because the holes are there."

"You give it a whirl and if it doesn't work out, I'll help you."

When I was done, it looked like a butthole.

TBG, in the truest sense of the word, was impressed. "Wow, you really do suck."

Okay, I digress. I know where my skills end. I ordered face masks and they came in today. The picture looked like good quality masks. The reality is, eight masks were all stored into a 5x7 pouch (red flag #1); when TBG pulled them out, it looked like he was peeling apart black Philo dough (red flag #2); and as soon as he peeled one off, I could see through it (and we're done). The dang thing barely fit over his face. Soooo...we now have panty liners for face masks I'll never make.

Dinner was another "Adventures of Eating with Bianca." Tonight was roasted veggie farro bowls (yep, Hello Fresh saves the day again). Mom decides it's lesson time. "Some children do not have the options you have, and would be over the moon to have all this food." This is the modern twist to the "children are starving in China" lecture.

Bianca just gives me her famous eye roll. Ahhh, but she is not prepared for Mom to turn it up a bit. "Tonight we're going to watch an educational film on countries that are starving." They're both curious as to what that exactly means.

After dinner, I get on and try to find a documentary on Third World countries. Apparently, they also have to include something about killing. We nixed that idea. We did find one on food waste and an experiment a couple did for six months. They challenged themselves to only live on what they could find for free. Poof! Like that, two kids were in awe of how much good food is thrown away daily. (It really was shocking). Brady has now determined we need to go dumpster diving for our food. I just wanted them to eat their damn veggies.

Well, tomorrow starts a new week of remote learning. Brady is already moaning about it... and all is right with the world.

DAY 30
April 14, 2020

I think there was too much gravitational pull today. It was what I call a Monday-Tuesday, without coffee/tea/shake (fill in with your favorite wake-up drink). Kids were off-mark, we were off-mark. The dogs were probably the only ones on point. Hell, even the cat didn't hiss at Lilo.

Bianca "finishes" school at 1030. She thinks she's crafty by saying she's done and closing her computer all confident and matter-of-fact. Not. So. Fast. Child.

TBG doesn't miss a beat, "What about art?"

Miss Confident shoots back, "I'll do it tomorrow."

He's not lettering her off that easy. "Spanish?"

"Tomorrow."

I come in as back-up, "Nope... have a seat and let's get on it."

Bianca gives her famous eye roll. (It's a genetic trait.) I think her face is going to freeze in that expression eventually.

Neither of them could sit still all day. I felt like I was playing the real life version of whack-a-mole.

"Brady, sit... Dad asked Bianca for help, not you."

"Bianca, stop twirling when we're talking."

"Brady, what are you staring at? Homework, please."

"Bianca, are there jumping beans in your pants?"

"Brady... Brady... Brraaddyyy!"

Day 30

The whole day was either bouncing everywhere or some sassy response to anything TBG or I said.

I am a root-cause type of gal. "You're all off-focus and can't sit still...it must be because you went to bed later last night. You're both in bed early tonight."

Ha! Whether it was or wasn't, the reason was a moot point. They both agreed (score one for Power of Suggestion) and Mommy and Daddy had a few more minutes of quiet time. Okay, okay, not true...we had a few more minutes to catch up on work we couldn't do today because we were busy chasing Tigger and Taz high on a case of Mountain Dew... with extra sugar.

I am *so* happy there is always a tomorrow after today.

DAY 31
April 15, 2020

We were back in the school-telework saddle today! For the most part...

Brady is a super-smart kid. Yes, of course we say that because we're his parents, but there is also truth in it. From watching him, you would never guess his read/retain ability is through the roof. Teachers have commented in the past that it looks like he is spacing out in class, but when they ask a question, he usually has the right answer. This high retention results in about 17 hours a day of fun facts.

"Did you know platypus are mammals that lay eggs?" (Knew that!)

"Did you know people from New Zealand are called Kiwis?" (Knew that!)

"Did you know if you pull apart antimatter it will come back together with greater force?" (Ummmm...)

He finds all his school courses interesting. What he doesn't find interesting is spelling. The child is as phonetic as it gets. My theory is that his brain is so full he has no room for proper spelling. At least 5-6 times a day we get the "how do you spell" question, and every time we tell him the same thing.

"Mom, how do you spell dream?"

"Sound it out."

"J.R.E.E.M."

TBG, Bianca, and me in unison: "What?!"

Making sure I heard right, I ask, "Did you say J?" All three of us are laughing at this point. Don't worry, this family prides itself on a little jeering, and his phonetic spelling ability has always been a humorous topic.

Brady sheepishly smiles, "It sounds like it... jrrreeemmm."

"Child... we need to check and see if you're blood-related to Auntie Jen." Auntie Jen has been my best friend since kindergarten, and she cannot spell to save her life.

Dictionary in Christmas stocking, check.

I'm a tea person. Always have been, always will be. Living in England for 3½ years only reinforced my love. This morning it was forty-I-can't-feel-my-legs-four degrees on our morning walk (don't judge...the northern girl has thin blood now), and I came in and immediately put the kettle on. The food waste documentary is stuck in my head, and they talked about reusing tea bags for a second or third cup of tea. I figured, good idea. When I lived in England, my British friends often did that. So on my second cup I reuse the tea bag. Hmmmmm...the difference in taste is like going from a Perrier to dishwater. Definitely not my cup of tea (pun intended). Sorry, Bev and Jerry (our British friends), I'm going to be a tea-bag waster for the rest of my life.

Kiddos actually get down to business today, get their work done...and actually do pretty well. This means that TBG and I also get work done during daylight hours. In the words of Charlie Sheen, *Winning!*

One of the blessings that has come out of all this madness is actually having the energy to cook dinner, having time to eat dinner, AND having conversation while eating dinner... every night. (Check back in a month, but for now it's a blessing.)

Now Brady, my darling boy, is just that... a boy. He can't tell a story without trying to relate it to bathroom humor. All. The. Time. Even better if he can put a farting noise to it. I also need to mention here that TBG, before we had

children, used to tell me all the time that guys think bathroom humor is funny. Famous last words, buddy...

Brady was at it again at dinner tonight.

TBG wasn't having it. "Dude, we're eating dinner. You don't have to turn every story into bathroom humor."

"Sorry, Dad."

I can't resist. I have to stoke the fire a teeny bit. "I've determined it's a gender trait." Then I reminded our darling son of his first grade bathroom adventure, which got him in a bit of trouble with the Vice

Principal. Now, as tempting as it is to tell the story, I'm respecting his privacy. However, if you run into Brady, ask him. Both kids were cracking up by this point, and TBG just shook his head, remembering his famous last words.

I continued, "What blew my mind was when I told a female about what you did, and they responded with the same surprise as I did. But when I told a guy, they cracked up laughing, almost reminiscing. Heck, one guy asked me if you played *Star Wars!*"

TBG is now smirking... probably also reminiscing.

I concluded my thesis, "So my point is validated: bathroom humor is a male gender trait."

Brady is giggling and grinning ear to ear, while shoveling food in his mouth, and proudly shouts, "YEP!"

"And yet, somehow y'all manage to find females to marry you." I said in disbelief.

After dinner, Brady had to practice his clarinet. He was a bit mopey about it, so to avoid procrastination, I told him I would practice with him.

I played the flute back in the day, and was pretty good at it. It's been a minute or two, but I can still make a noise and remember most of my fingerings. So, we have at it; minus sounding a little airy (if you call a wind tunnel a "little windy"), forgetting what an A flat was, losing my place on the music 20 times (and making him start over every time)... I didn't do too bad. When we were done, Brady pipes up, "You're a little rusty, but it sounded pretty good."

"Next time, start with the compliment before stating reality, my darling child."

"Oops," he giggles.

I find our high school graduation song, "Friends." I decide to give it a whirl while the kiddos get ready for bed. (They're all excited because they're sleeping in their fort tonight.)

I hear Brady talking to TBG. "Mom is rusty, but I'm going to have her keep practicing with me, and she'll get better."

Hells bells, now I'm his music project. Lol... hope he's ready. We'll let you know when the concert date is set.

DAY 32
April 16, 2020

I needed to go to the clinic today to get dental paperwork signed for my upcoming R.E.T.I.R.E.M.E.N.T. Holy crapolly, just saying the word "retirement" comes with a ton of mixed emotions. I'm not even sure how to describe it: joy, relief, and frustration are the three that pop in my head first. It's still six months away, so not worth dwelling on too much, as I have a ton to get done before them.

This is my first trip out of the house on my own since lockdown. You would have thought I was going to prom. I not only showered, but I also actually dried and flat-ironed my hair (my version of styling) and put foundation and Chapstick on. Woot woot... Cinderella is ready for the ball!

While I was pretending I was in a spa shower, one little girl snuck in and left me a surprise... a smoothie made by her. First thought: "Awww", followed by "Hmmmm...what's she buttering me up for?"

As I come down the stairs, Bianca is sitting on the couch snuggling our geriatric dog, Amelia. She looks up and with a big grin says, "Mommy, did you like your surprise?"

"It was amazing! Thank you... did you make it?"

"Yes!" Then without missing a beat. "Hey 'Mommy guess what? I had a poop fart today."

"Did you check your pants?"

"Yes, I threw my undies in my hamper."

My inside voice, *Gross*; my outside voice, "How did that happen?"

"Well I think it was because of the smoothie... it made my poop all liquid."

"Naturally," now wondering what I was in for.

I head out on my solo adventure; praying the smoothie did not have the same effect on me. I was excited to jam with XM radio on my Roadtrip Rock Tour, starring me. This is only second to my Shower Jams Rock Tour. The only weird part was wearing my mask. (Remember those panty-liner thin masks we bought? Yeah, needs must, I'm wearing it.) I felt and looked like the Hamburgler with really long hair. The trip was definitely surreal and made me hope this was not becoming our new norm.

When I got home, the kids had finished homework and got outside to bike around. We took advantage and soaked up some vitamin sun while watching them zoom around. Remember being a kid and putting cards in our spokes? Well, the kids took it to a new level...a piece of a plastic bottle in the spokes. Now they all sound like mini drifter cars.

Bianca comes flying by, "Mommy, watch this!" Riding with one hand, she lost a little control and bumped into the curb. "Ow, my nuts!"

"You don't have those, girl," Really curious why I have to remind the daughter of a nurse about her genital parts.

"Oh, right. Ow, my hoohah."

"There ya go."

As the kids are brushing their teeth before bed, Brady pops downstairs, eager to share his new observation. "Hey Dad! Here's something cool. You know how plaque gets in your teeth and you use floss to get it out?"

TBG, half-listening, "Ummm, yep."

"Well when it dries on the floss it gets really hard!"

TBG, now paying a bit more attention, "And you know this because…"

"Bianca flossed her teeth and put the floss back in the bag by mistake, instead of throwing it away. When I pulled one out it was her used one and the plaque was all hard! Cool!" (They use individual little flossers).

I'm sure I didn't hear right. "Wait, what did he say!?"

TBG validated me, "Yes, you heard right...she threw her used floss in the bag of clean ones."

"God bless, what is wrong with our children?"

On a good note, they got to sleep in their fort... so bedtime was a breeze.

Always find the silver lining.

DAY 33
April 17, 2020

It was Purple Up for school today. I was curious if Brady was going to be game for it. Yessiree! Both come down looking like some kind of kiddie rapper gang. Their teachers made a special video for the students. As we were watching, Brady points out that one of the teachers is his friend's Dad.

Me, thinking out loud, "Wouldn't it be cool if I taught at your school!?"

Bianca runs over and hugs me, "Yes!"

Brady has a bit of a worried smile, "Ummmm... no."

I couldn't resist, I had to play it up a little, "What!? Why?"

"Mom, just no."

"Awwwww."

We usually start the morning with some trampoline time. It burns some energy and gives me time to have a cup of tea (the real reason). Before they head out, I try to get their attention and talk to them about what school work needs to be done. Sigh... I would rather have tried to catch caffeinated squirrels.

On the 25th attempt and now raising my voice: "Hey, both of you... come over here now, please."

Bianca, standing at attention and rendering a salute, "Bianca reporting, Ma'am!"

Me giving her an eye roll, "Seriously?"

Brady is now attempting to be equally hilarious and throws a Beetle Bailey salute, giggling. "Ma'am, SSgt. Hoffmeyer reporting as ordered!"

"Sigh... just can't be normal, can we?"

We got the official word this afternoon that the kids would not be going back to school for the rest of this year. We held off on saying anything until we were able to tell them together. I'm confident it will be fine. I mention to TBG, "It's all good, I already prepped them a few weeks ago that this might happen."

'Okay, good."

A few hours later, we're getting dinner ready and they're playing on the trampoline. I thought it would be a good time to mention it to them. Remember, in my mind they would say "Okay" and keep jumping.

Me, talking out the kitchen window to them jumping on the trampoline, "Hey guys, can I have your attention for a minute?" Freeze frame... they both look toward me (well, that was better than this morning). I keep going, "The governor decided that no one is going back to school this year."

Bianca has an insta-meltdown. "I WON'T SEE MY FRIENDS...I MISS MY FRIENDS!" Throwing herself all over the trampoline. Emmy performance.

Brady keeps it simple: "That sucks."

These two, like any respectable siblings, fight like cats and dogs until one of them is hurting (physically or emotionally). Brady comes and gives Bianca a hug. "It's okay, Bianca." They truly amaze me.

Fortunately, the meltdown is short-lived. (Sweet baby Jesus, thank you!) We talk about it and although she's not keen on not seeing her friends, she understands why. We understand why too, and we both want to have our own meltdowns. Two of us teleworking, two kiddos remote learning, and me preparing for retirement; yeah, this oughta be fun times.

Brady joined the band this year. Remote learning has changed the game, and now we have the family band versus the school band. I thought it was a great way for TBG and I to get back into our instruments. Just before dinner, we go up and "play" our instruments with Brady - Brian, trumpet; Brady, clarinet; Bianca, cornet, and me, flute. God blessed, it's rough. I sound like a windbag, Brian forgets notes, Brady's new (he gets a pass). I actually

think Bianca, with no cornet experience, sounds better than us. Let me just say that I'm impressed the neighbors didn't throw rotten food at the house. We need a little practice.

Well, we made it to another Friday. TBG and I have wised up and let the kids keep the fort they put up earlier in the week. There's a specific reason for this. See, bedtime in our house is a cross between WWE meets Mr. Rogers, and usually takes 10 rituals and 24 good nights. (Okay, slightly exaggerated... but you get the point). Tonight, with the incentive of sleeping in the fort, it's only a quick whirl around the dance floor.

I'm pretty happy with ourselves, "This fort is a pretty smart idea! Bedtime is a breeze!"

"And that's why we're leaving it up," TBG announces.

"Clever... not bad for a sergeant."

"Jerkface."

"Heeheeheehee."

DAY 34
April 18, 2020

Lordy, it's been an insanely busy day.

TBG and I decide to walk the dogs, as our 57-pound black carpet (a.k.a. Lilo) is spazzing around the house at warp speed. However, it's a chilly Texas morning. Yes, we have those. For some reason that I have no explanation for, I always go to TBG and ask how cold it is. The same guy that has 100 pounds on me and wore cargo shorts in the middle of winter in Germany.

"Is it cold outside?"

"Not too bad... it's 50s out."

I step outside and step right back in. "Are you kidding me...? You must have forgotten the windchill factor!" I have no idea why I ask him; I never believe his assessment. I head back upstairs to put my lined workout pants on.

TBG laughs, "Seriously? We're walking a 90-year-old dog... we ain't going that fast."

"Exactly my point. I won't be breaking a sweat." As I'm putting on my sneakers, Lilo comes running over, turns around, and sits facing away from me. I look up and burst out laughing. You never realize how bad a job you did giving a haircut until it starts growing out. It looks like a lawnmower went part way and just gave up. I don't think our groomer will be impressed.

As I come downstairs, our garbage disposal, Brady, is eagerly waiting for me. "What's for breakfast?"

Without changing my expression: "Nothing. It's not your day to eat."

TBG chimes in on the razzing. "Remember, your days are Tues/Thurs and Bianca's are Mon/Weds."

The kids laugh, "Hey!"

As we're leaving for our walk, we tell the kids they have 15 minutes of TV and then they can grab something for breakfast. I'm certain we're coming home to the TV going and an "Ooops, we forgot!"

We get back, start to walk in the door, and are greeted with Bianca hollering, "CLOSE YOUR EYES!"

We just look at each other for a second. "Ummm, okay." We're both secretly assessing the situation. No smoke smell; good, not a fire. Okay, what evidence are they trying to quickly destroy? Two minutes later, we're allowed to walk into the kitchen, and we both stop in our tracks.

On the kitchen table were three plates filled with omelets, fruit, nuts, and olives and hot tea. There were four; Bianca was hungry and ate hers before we got back.

I have to explain why we're beyond impressed.

Brady is our child who thought someone was roasting marshmallows, when in reality it was a hot mitt smoldering in a drawer and he never went to check it out. If Brian hadn't walked back in the door, I'm sure the house would not exist right now (or worse).

Needless to say, we're a bit cautious when it comes to kids cooking unattended. Andddd... hence why I'm happy and seriously relieved the house is still standing.

Bianca is so excited to tell us, "Mommy I made you the omelet!"

"Mom, I supervised Bianca to make sure she didn't burn anything. And I cleaned up everything."

Sweet baby Jesus... we died and went to parent heaven! They must want something really big; with a surprise like that, they could probably pull it off. We'll keep that our secret.

After a day of rearranging the entire upstairs. Bianca asks me to come upstairs and practice music with her. I grab my flute. That's not her plan.

"No, Mommy, I'm going to teach you how to play the piano."

"Ohhhh, gotcha." Well, hell, she has 10 more piano lessons than me... I'm sure she can teach me something. Twenty minutes later, I am now a master of *Jingle Bells*.

We decide to put Messenger Kids on their tablets. Maybe it's because we're older parents that we're careful with too much of any technology. We've heard too many horror stories of zombie children, and with an ADHD child, we stay vigilant of his affinity to lose himself in such things as technology. So, Messenger has lots of parental controls, and we likey. They spend the rest of the time catching up with friends and family.

Brady, all excited to talk to anyone: "Mom, can I call Miss Johnny?"

"Sure."

Five minutes into their conversation, Brady wants to show her their coin collection, and I chat with her while he runs upstairs to grab it.

Besides already looking like a weekend Medusa, I am now looking at myself rocking glitter-gold glasses with a matching headband and lipstick. My girlfriend is getting a good chuckle. Messenger Kids has a number of faces/disguises to play with. We agree we needed to use this app for our remote office meetings.

"This is way more fun! I was a jester talking to my Mom and Dad, and some sort of bird horse talking to my nephew. I think the unicorn would be perfect for staff meetings!"

Johnny laughs. "We might actually pay attention to what's being said."

Cleaning house is, by far, my least favorite job. My first actual job where taxes were taken out was cleaning the local motel down the road from my parent's house. I hated every minute of it. I used to sit on the bed and watch TV to vacuum whatever was within the reach of the vacuum. It was also one of the motivators for me to go to college. So I guess some good came out of it. Now, as an adult, I will clean because I hate a dirty house more. However, I clean to a level above toxic but well below sterile. I'm sure my Mom is disappointed. As we're in the midst of our "below sterile" cleaning today, I find a family journal... void of any journaling. I know exactly who would be thrilled to have this.

"Bianca, look what I found for you."

"Thank you, Mommy!" and off she runs to immediately start filling it.

At bedtime we have two special events: a lost tooth (I swear she ripped it out) and the first page of *Pandemic Parodies, Kid's Edition* was written. Let's talk about this tooth. I'm a nurse. I've seen blood, guts, vomit, excrement, urine, and had my hand in places that should never be mentioned. Bottom line, I've got a pretty strong stomach... except when it comes to teeth. I have no idea what it is about a tooth being pulled, but it makes me squirm just thinking about it. Then I have a child who thinks pulling a tooth is awesome. As soon as she feels a tooth starting to loosen up she's on it, working it until she can pull it out. Ugh...that last time she did, that it took about a year for the new tooth to come in.

As I'm coming in to tuck her in for bed, I see her working away in her journal. She looks up and gives me a big toothless smile. "Mommy, I'm writing a kid's version of the *Pandemic Parodies!*" I smirk. That girl is nothing short of amazing. I think it might be a bestseller.

DAY 35
April 19, 2020

I've been a little off-kilter the last couple days. Snappy (I'd rather refer to it as *extra witty*), a bit shorter-fused, tired, not wanting to be social. Ladies, I know ya get me. This morning I showed some of my extra witty charm to TBG.

"You're awful saucy today. How about I talk to you again in seven days?"

"Shut it," I snap, as I give him the death stare.

Bianca comes bopping down the stairs. "Mommy, the tooth fairy came. She gave me $2... all in quarters." (Slightly annoyed tone)

"Well, maybe she wants you to be able to make change for people."

Brady chimes in, "Or maybe so you could share it with me!"

TBG doesn't miss a beat, "Freeloader."

I look over at our darling eldest. "Brady, what are you wearing?"

He gives me a big goofy grin. "Papa's PJ bottoms. I found them in my closet! Papa said to keep them for him, for when he comes back."

"Papa is not going to want them after your stinky butt has been in them."

"HAHAHAHAHA... you know it!"

We chill most of the day and work on various hobbies. Bianca and I are working on a project where you make a picture with microscopic beads. I've never worked on something that was so infuriating and satisfying at the same time. The coding is ridiculous... it's a teeny-colored dot with a symbol inside it. The color and symbol match the key that has a number on it, which tells you which bead to use. (Confused yet?) Everything is so damn tiny, a freaking magnifying glass still doesn't help. If an optometrist wanted to give a thorough eye exam, this would be the way to go.

We're making a panda in a cherry tree. There are 4,000 different colored beads in nonsequential order...pure torture. Since I am apparently slightly masochistic, I keep working on it.

"Bianca, which bead is this symbol?"

Bianca sighs, all exasperated. "Use the magnifying glass, Mommy."

"It doesn't help me."

Bianca sighs, looks for 0.1 seconds and says, "It's this one," and goes skipping off.

Under my breath, "Turd."

Since it's a beautiful day, I think I'll sit outside and enjoy the weather while I work on the sadistic beading project. Brady is working with his kid pottery wheel, attempting to make a shot glass for Dad. For a brief second, this does have me mildly worried that we're not sending them the right message. Meh, he's focused and quiet; we'll call it good. Point three seconds after I set myself up, Bianca roams outside. You can just see the trouble brewing in her eyes. And she strikes...

"Bianca, leave my clay alone!"

"What? I just want a little piece."

"DON'T, BIANCA... LEAVE IT ALONE!"

"But I want to make a panda."

My inside voice, *Just five freaking minutes,* translated to my outside voice, "Both of you, knock it off!"

Brady, completely annoyed and not interested in battling with her, says, "I'm going on the trampoline." It may only be 10 feet from the patio, but at least they're separated and quiet. Deep breath... back to my damn beads I can't see.

Five seconds later, Brady decides he has to improv a rendition of Tarzan by screaming at the top of his lungs as he jumps as high

as possible. I am quickly losing my mind. "Brady, it's supposed to be peaceful out here, not sound like a battle cry competition!"

"Sorry, Mom."

God blessed, so much for a relaxing and frustrating afternoon of my sadistic bead project.

Day 35

My husband is a pretty awesome cook. One of his specialties is banana waffles. Brady scarfed four this morning! I've tried a thousand times, but they never come out, so I concede that he is the Waffle King. Now when we are talking bread... weeelll ... that is a whole different story.

TBG has been attempting to make bread the last couple days, with little success. Now, in his defense, he's using gluten-free flour. (However, I made a batch of gluten-free rolls last week and they were A.W.E.S.O.M.E... just saying.) Anyway, it's been a rough go. Today, he tried to make ekmek (a Turkish version of naan). He ran into the same problem again; it would barely rise. It came out okayish... kind of like eating softened cardboard. But it wasn't too shabby with honey and butter.

The kids love pretzel rolls. We usually buy them from the grocery store, but with all this chaos going on, they're a bit harder to get. I get a recipe from my cousin Julie and decide I'm going to give it a whirl. Yeah, I'm pretty good at this.

"Dang, look how much the dough rose," I brag.

"You're just going to rub this in my face, aren't you?" TBG shoots back.

"Well, not intentionally. Good is just good." I smile.

Fourteen minutes later, the house smells like baking bread.

"OMG, they smell amazing!" I just cannot help being impressed with myself.

He's so not impressed.

"Oooo.. . they came out perfect... soft and fluffy," I continue.

"I so cannot deal with you." And in the next breath he blurts, "You're going to share one with me, right?"

"Of course I'll share my perfection with you."

"You are so freaking arrogant."

"Jealous. Here, babe... I even buttered it for you," handing him a warm buttered pretzel roll.

He takes a bite. "Okay, you're the Bread Queen."

"Why, yes I am."

Day 35

DAY 36
April 20, 2020

Well, we're still at it. Monday starts off as one would expect for a Monday. School Hoffmeyer starts promptly at 1000-ish as I remembered a meeting I had to be in 30 minutes before it started, and darted upstairs with a cup of tea and protein bar.

The kids have been fort-sleeping in Brady's room, and it has its pros and cons. Upside, bedtime is a snap and they're getting along well. Downside, they conspire more together. The other night they apparently were faking sleep and partied like rock stars until late. Of course, it totally bit them in the butt when they were walking around like zombies the next day, with Brady submitting half his work because he didn't read all the directions. Sometimes ya just have to learn the hard way.

This morning they came downstairs all proud of themselves. They wrote a breakfast menu for TBG and I, so we could pick and they would make us breakfast later this week. Who abducted my children and replaced them with these pod-people?! Never mind, I'd like to keep these models. I made sure I picked the cold dishes. I'll take my chances on a cut finger over a burned-down house.

TBG had to go on base and had to leave about 30 minutes before I was done with my meeting. You know what that means... cue the chaos.

Like clockwork, arguments start. One wants to make a smoothie in the really loud blender. (Please wait until my meeting is over.) One wants help with homework. (Of course you do.) The dog is chasing the cat, the cat is chasing the dog. I start and stop my email 30 times.

I finally get off the meeting, feed the kiddos, help with homework, get everyone settled with an activity. Sigh... okay, I try to get back to my email. Fifteen minutes later, Brady comes in from the backyard.

"Mom, one of the dogs threw up out here on the cement."

"Okay, just get the hose and wash it off."

Back to my email. The kids are now back inside, reading and finishing homework, and 10 minutes later we all hear a quick gushing noise. We look over. Lilo threw up again, this time on the carpet. Dammit, the gods hate me today.

Captain Obvious pipes up, "Ugh, it was Lilo that threw up outside."

Miss Quizzical needs the details. "How do you know?"

"Because they both have carrots and cat poop in them." Lilo's and Amelia's favorite pastime is cleaning out the cat litter box for us. I'm turning green listening to his description.

I clean up the cat poop, carrot puke and am thankful for a strong nurse's stomach.

Okay...attempt #4583, back to my email. Whatever; my attempts just bring on more distraction. TBG comes home... more distraction. We get grade alerts from Brady's teacher; trying to figure out why... more distraction.

Two blessed hours later, I finally send my email! And that's my only success of the day.

I head outside for a breather and chat with the kids. As I turn to head back inside, something hits me. It is freaking bird poop! How in the world did I get hit, where there's a mesh screen over our pergola!? That damn thing has some serious thrust and accuracy!

I walk in the house defeated. Monday won.

TBG comes through and brings home a little chocolate for me. Consolation prize for my manic, pukey, shi#^y Monday.

Day 36

DAY 37
April 21, 2020

Screw Taco Tuesday, it's Take 'Em Down Tuesday.

Somedays, life with a child with ADHD can become a challenge both for him and us. Always harder for the kiddo, especially when he's giving it his all. Today is one of those days.

Honestly, both of them look like they have ants in their pants most of the day. They've decided this is going to be the morning they're going to play "restaurant." It's awesome, until I become the recipient of the half-cooked omelet with cheese, Tabasco, and salsa. Not a lover of runny eggs, nor Tabasco or salsa on my eggs; and yet, I feel obliged to set an example.

Bianca, looking distraught; "Mommy, sorry we mixed up your order with Daddy's."

"No worries, just give me Daddy's."

"Ummm, he has salsa and Tabasco too."

My inside voice hollers, *Gross!* However, my outside voice sucked it up, "Okay then" (taking a bite...yep gross). "That's pretty good!" It's not a total lie if it's not the best or worst I had, right? Also me... secretly tossing eggs in the garbage when they weren't looking.

The rest of my day went something like this: "Brady, sit down and start your work."

"Bianca, he doesn't need to see your mini clay animal right now."

"Brady, she doesn't need your help."

"Bianca, leave your brother alone."

"No, we don't need music blaring."

"Bianca, save the Macarena for later."

"Brady, we can buy more clay, let her use the clay."

"Brady... back to your work."

"Brady, are you sure you turned it in? Check again. Ahhhh... see? Pays to double-check your work."

I might have been more successful talking to the bad@$$ reflection in the mirror.

We end the evening practicing our instruments, thinking this will be a nice way to wind down for the night. Nope, we're not there quite yet... hold tight. Brady looks like he is nearly levitating during our practice. I am seriously considering putting cement boots on him. After 500 more redirections, we finish practice and get ready for bed. Let's hope a good night's sleep settles them down. Phew... if not, Nana or Oma may get surprise FedEx deliveries.

DAY 38
April 22, 2020

After two less than awesome days, we finally get back on track today.

Lilo has her groomer's appointment. Lordy, does she need it. The groomer's assistant called yesterday to remind us she had an appointment. I wouldn't have missed that appointment for the world! God knows what the poor dog would look like if we had to give her one of our creative clips again.

As excited as I am for this appointment, I'm a little worried our groomer will disown us for the jacked-up attempt at grooming her ourselves. But then I figure she'll be understanding in our current pandemic state. Nonetheless, I feel I have to fess up before we bring her there, for fear they'll call the Humane Society on us.

Me on the phone with the groomer: "I need to let you know she's a hot mess."

"It's all good."

"No, see, she had surgery two weeks ago and has her legs shaved for IVs."

"Not a big deal."

"And we clipped her ourselves because it was getting hot out and we couldn't get in sooner with you. So, she kind of looks like a lawnmower randomly attacked her."

The office manager cracks up laughing. "Oh! I'll go let her know right now."

I knew it. That dog would have been on the late-night infomercial for the nonprofit for mistreated dogs if I hadn't explained. That was worse than church confession.

Deena is the owner and groomer extraordinaire at Greener Grooming LLC. She meets me outside with a big smile (well, I'm suspecting a smile under the mask because she's nice), to pick up our Rastafarian carpet. I refrain from apologizing again for our pseudo-grooming attempt. She sees the evidence; enough said.

Five hours later, a very refined-looking poodle comes walking out the door. TBG goes and picks her up, and thinks Deena brought out the wrong dog! When they get home, the cat thinks we brought home a new dog and starts hissing at her. Pretty sure Lilo lost 20 pounds.

The kiddos rock out school today. Thank goodness they're more on the independent side today. Both TBG and I handled phone call after phone call. Of course, I handled it in pure Mom fashion... multitasking.

Here's a perfect example of guys versus gals when it comes to multitasking. TBG is on the phone handling business. I'm on the phone, also handling business, while making pretzel bread for dinner (the minions devoured the first batch already), sending emails, and shooing kids away who mysteriously need to immediately know the Earth's gravitational pull on the third Tuesday of the month. I would also like to add that they never ask *him* these questions when he's busy, only me. Grrrrrr...

TBG has full homeschooling duties the next two days, as I get the pleasure of a day-and-a-half telecon. (Please send prayers.) Hope he's taken some notes on Mom's multitasking style. He's gonna need it.

Since the wee ones are done early, they want to hand out their random acts of kindness gifts to the neighborhood kids. Bianca made these teeny tiny figures of various animals and painted them.

"Mommy, I want to show you what I made. You guess what animal they are."

My inside voice: *Oh boy, I'm sure I'll have zero idea.* My outside voice ignores my inside voice. "Sure!"

My inside voice was right, it didn't go so awesome:

Pink blob, "Bunny?"

Bianca is disappointed, "No, Puma."

Blue blob, "Dog."

"No, hyena."

Gold blob, "Gold Finger!"

Bianca is really not impressed. "No, coyote."

Grey blob with gold Mohawk, "Horse!"

No, unicorn!"

Black and gray blob: "Panda!"

Bianca, relieved I am not a total idiot, "Yes!"

Phew, I'm redeemed. Twelve blobs later, I got a total of 2 right. Glad she's a forgiving kid.

It's a day of giving and receiving. Oma sent a few masks for us. Sweet! And a very sweet friend left a goodie bag. Now, it said it was for the Hoffmeyers... but based on the items (tea, face mask, bath bomb) it was obviously mostly geared for Mom (muhahaha). Brady thought we got bubble bath.

I just looked at him in awe, "Did you read the label?"

"Yes... it said multi-surface cleaner. Our skin is a surface and it was pink."

The child is some kind of special. It is a small bottle of Lysol cleaner.

And on that note, I am so thankful we are on the downside of the week. Embrace the good, bad, ugly and zany...we're all in this together!

DAY 39
April 23, 2020

The adventure today: HEB! (For those not in Central Texas... the mecca of all grocery stores). As I'm getting a grocery list together, TBG asks Alexa to put on the '80s one-hit wonders. Then proceeds to ask me at every song, "Guess who sings this?".

And every time I answer the same, "No idea."

TBG names some obscure band and then says, "Alexa, who sings this song?"; and then does a little arm pump, high five to the air when he gets it right.

We're hitting a new low here.

TBG, as the next one-hit wonder comes on, says, "Name this artist."

"Seriously... I can't even remember *my* name most days."

I haven't been in any grocery store for probably 6 months for 2 reasons...1) Prior to COVID, time was limited with both of us working, and delivery was a saving grace; 2) The first month of stay-at-home orders I was still recovering from the flu and couldn't shake the crud.

Between not knowing where anything was anymore and enamored with all the various choices (especially the three aisles of wine), I was like a kid at a carnival.

Three hours and $455 later, I finished. I start to load the groceries onto the belt and remember to pull out my reusable bags. The cashier stops for a moment, "Um Ma'am...if you are going to use your own bags, you have to bag your own groceries." Damn COVID, I forgot businesses went to disposable everything.

"No problem." Total lie. I have $455 worth of groceries...this is going to be a pain in the backside. As I'm paying, I remember another bonus of delivery... no impulse buying. I rationalize that it'd been 2½ weeks, and I'm stocking up. Sounds legit to me.

I take so long, (because I had to bag my own) TBG thinks I made a mad dash for the border.

When I get home, the kids are running out to play. Brady comes running out the door, "Mom, we painted! It's out back."

"Sweet!"

I walk in and I am hit by spray paint fumes... and I'm confused. Were they making graffiti art?

TBG, all proud of himself, "I spray-painted my nerf gun."

"You really are getting bored, eh?"

"Yep."

Bianca brings me outside to show off the paintings they created earlier today.

"Mommy, guess!"

Oh boy, I'm still traumatized by the clay figurines. "Burrito, Hamburger, Boat, and I have no idea (no use lying)."

"That's a dinosaur, another dinosaur, and a meteor."

"Ahhhh...of course," relieved that I got at least 3 out of 4.

We have dinner tonight, and Sweet Baby Jesus, Bianca eats it. It isn't her favorite, but she eats it and doesn't go for a second Guinness World Record for the longest time to eat dinner. Woot woot... we're making progress!

We get the kiddos to bed (still winning with the fort) and ten minutes later TBG, like a giddy kid on Christmas with his new toy, says, "Want to see what my angel eyes look like?" Yes, the same car lights he was trying to show me before.

"I think you need an intervention."

"You can just stand at the door and look."

"Oh, okay... I'll even go outside for you."

He turns the lights on with a big grin, happy with his work.

"Nice lights. Do they wink?"

"You're not right."

Day 39

DAY 40
April 24, 2020

I really didn't think I'd still be writing this. Specifically, I didn't think my family could give comedic relief this many days in a row. Yet here I am, still winning it.

Last night, Bianca started complaining of a tummy ache. I hoped a good night's sleep would do the trick. No such luck.

"Mommy, my tummy still hurts."

"Okay, lay on the couch and watch a show."

TBG and I have to run to Lowes, so we ask Brady to keep an eye on her.

About 15 minutes into shopping (looking at toilet seat covers of all things), TBG and I hear a "thud"... and see a gentleman face-first on the ground, moaning. The weight of the box he was carrying shifted forward, sending him down. As soon as I see him going down, I sprint over, praying it isn't a heart attack. Someone has called 911 for me and is trying to relay messages.

Realizing he isn't medical, I gently say, "Might be easier if I talk to Dispatch."

The guy doesn't hesitate. "Good idea."

Dispatch asks the COVID questions and then says, "Please make sure you do not give him food or water."

As I'm looking around the toilet seat/vacuum aisle at Lowe's, I'm thinking, *Right, ummm, we're on the floor in the vacuum aisle at Lowes...don't think it will be an issue.*

Fortunately, it ended up being only a bloody lip and possibly a strained (maybe cracked) rib. Either way, it wasn't a heart attack, stroke, or seizure (all of which I was dreading) and he'll make a full recovery.

One minute later, Bianca calls. "Mommy, I threw up a bit."

"Do you feel better?"

"A little."

Brady jumps on the phone, "Mom! I was going to make her some Senna tea so she could poop out everything and feel better."

"That's a nice thought, but might not be a good idea with an upset tummy."

"Yeah, she said, 'No thank you'... so I made her some Sleepytime tea instead."

"Very nice, kiddo/" (phew.)

We finally start shopping, and TBG needs outdoor outlets. I need to explain why this is funny. This guy hates to do anything with electricity. It stems back to his medic days when he took care of a patient or two who worked on the powerlines and were the recipients of a volt or two. So, when he decides he has to do anything related to power, I know it will be a national event and he has to shut the city down... just to be safe.

When we finally got home, two hours later, Bianca was still on the couch looking a bit under the weather. I brought her upstairs to take a bath, then just let her flop on the couch. About an hour later,

Bianca runs into the kitchen smiling from ear to ear. "Mommy. I feel so much better!"

"You do!? Wow.. good."

"Yah, I farted!"

So glad I wasn't in that room. And after that, what is there to say...?

DAY 41
April 25, 2020

Well, Monday came in with a swoop. The kids are getting back into school rhythm, and TBG and I are sorting out the morning on who has meetings when. I win the short straw for the meetings. (Dammit!) TBG runs the homeschooling front. It's a toss-up on who really got the short stick, depending on who has to deal with the most chaos. Let the fun begin!

I'm taking the opportunity to have a cup of tea before my first meeting while listening to the kids jumping on the trampoline. Out of the blue we hear a very off-tune version of *Danny Boy* belted out at the top of Brady's lungs.

TBG, shaking his head, "WTH is wrong with our child?"

"You got me," I mindlessly say, as I'm more focused on enjoying my tea.

I have zero idea what goes on in our house for most of the day, as I spend the day upstairs between meetings and work projects. What I do know is I only hear crying twice and neither of them is blood-curdling; there are no signs of TBG day-drinking; and the house does not look like a tornado hit it... so I'd say a pretty damn good day!

Bianca's birthday is three days away, and of course she has ensured we do not forget. "Three days until my birthday, Mommy!"

"Yes, baby."

"Just want you to know."

At dinner I mention I'm going to make a practice cake.

Bianca makes sure she gets her order in. "I want a chocolate cake with sprinkles IN the cake."

Brady shoots back, "She didn't say the cake was for you."

Bianca glares at him.

TBG chimed in, "Ooooh, good one... you've been served!"

This family is relentless.

We settle down for the night and TBG finds an "educational" show on Amazon Prime. Did you know sea cucumbers breathe out of their butts and have little fish that not only crawl in the sea cucumber's butthole for protection, but also mate there and eat their gonads and poop? No? Well, now you do. You're welcome.

After a riveting and inspiring educational show, we send the kiddos up to brush their teeth and go to bed. Ten minutes later Brady walks downstairs and fesses up that they were fooling around and cut each other's hair.

"You what?" I have no idea why I would be shocked at this statement.

TBG obviously has to know why. "Why in God's name would you decide that is a remotely intelligent thing to do?!"

"Well, she let me." (And there's your intelligent answer, TBG.)

"And Brady let me cut his." (And another one...)

I'm just wondering if there's a bottle of wine already open in the fridge.

Brady, in full defense mode blurts out, "At least I told you!"

Well, there's that...the desperate and only move he had.

So now they both have a top section on the top of their head chopped up. Apparently we need more *Danny Boy* sung on the trampoline.

Oh Donna girl, the wine, the wine is calling...

Day 41

DAY 42
April 26, 2020

This morning I'm walking into the kitchen listening to TBG explaining the variety of subjects that make up humanities to Brady. Somewhere in there, I hear TBG bring up Bikini Atoll and Brady comes back with, "Oh yeah, the nuclear testing site."

I do a double-take. "Wait a minute... you can't remember if you put on underwear any given day, but randomly know Bikini Atoll?"

"Interesting facts, Mom."

"I think knowing if you have underwear on would be an interesting fact."

I'm trying to get my day started (a.k.a., turn the computer on) and have a cup of tea, while the kiddos start in on schoolwork. I'm busy reading an email, half-listening to what's going on around me. (I have to say this, as it will be my defense for my next comment.)

Bianca asks, "Mommy, who was the second president?"

"Ummm, Lincoln." (See above.)

Brady looks at me in horror. "Ummm, John Adams, Mom."

"I was just making you feel good."

Brady gives me the "whatever" look. "You had no clue."

"Get on your homework." (Yeah, so there.)

I swear they're getting faster with their homework. The first week we were drowning; now I wonder if we should secretly ask the teachers to turn it up a teeny bit. (No, not really... I don't want to answer any more questions). Third-grade math already threw me for a loop today. How hard can it be to count blocks to determine area? Well, I'm here to tell you, it's damn hard. It's a sad day when you go through the step-by-step and still can't follow the logic. Naturally it's the damn system... no way I wouldn't know third-grade math. Nope... no way.

The kids take off upstairs to go play, and all is right for about an hour... until there's a bloodcurdling scream, a door slam, and a frustrated Brady walking downstairs. "What's up, kiddo?"

"I wanted to use Lift as an attack, and she keeps telling me no."

Okay, so they've made their knock-off version of Pokémon... they call it Pikimon (or something to that effect). They're developing their own player cards.

As we're talking, a teary-eyed little girl comes downstairs, and she turns red in the face and bursts into tears, trying to tell me her version. Let me just say the reaction was WAY over the top for the situation. TBG and I just look at each other.

TBG, whispering to me, "WTH... ummm, you notice these events seem to coincide with a monthly cycle? Just saying."

"Sigh, yep." There's no denying it.

And so I somehow try to explain to an almost-nine-year-old that it's not really her fault that her head is spinning and she's talking in demonic voices in reaction to a minor situation. "Bianca, sometimes you may feel like you want to rip someone's head off, but not understand why you feel like it."

"I feel like I want to burn a house down."

"Well, yep, that's legit too. Boy, Mom can't wait for the teen years... woohoo, they're gonna be fun!" (Shit, we spawned Satan's offspring.)

Bianca, head now positioned correctly, giggles, gives me a big hug, and runs outside to play.

TBG just looks at me in awe. "There are no words."

"Well, there's a little foreshadowing for us."

Of course, the kids were raring for more educational shows. Tonight we learned male penguins hire prostitutes (paid for in stones), some female fish fake orgasms when they're with a subpar male, some crabs eat their partners after mating, and garter snakes have orgies.

"Mom, what's a prostitute?" Ugh, why do they always ask me the mortifying questions?

"It's a girlfriend you pay for."

"Mom, what's an orgasm?" God blessed…

"When your privates are really happy."

"Mom, what's an orgy?" They apparently have forgotten they have a Dad who answers questions too.

"It's a party with a lot of people hugging each other."

"Awwww... fun!"

TBG is doing his best to not burst out laughing.

Yep... questions I never wanted to answer, and more information you never wanted to know about animal mating. Again, you're welcome.

DAY 45
April 29, 2020 (Who stole Monday and Tuesday?)

It's Birthday Eve today for one almost-nine-year-old, and the excitement seems to be causing all kinds of overreactions. The most noteworthy event is getting her video biography done. Sweet baby Jesus....

For starters, our little girl is trying to whip through her report. Since I'm the Mom model with that built-in "you're BS-ing me" sixth sense, I double-check the homework and find out she needs to do a video for her report. "Bianca, you might want to read those instructions again."

"No, Mom, I'm good." This is to become my new first name: "No, Mom." Alas, my words got to her. She reluctantly looks and nonchalantly states, "Oh, okay... I see now."

"Uh huh... I don't just make this stuff up."

She decides she's going to make the setting a newsroom and Amelia is her co-anchor. We're hoping both Amelia and Lilo will be game, but Lilo isn't having it. As she is setting up, Bianca bumps her knee, which causes her already scabbed wound to bleed. This sets off a dang five-alarm meltdown and she is full-on blubbering. I, seeing that she's not anywhere near death, and knowing this will go on forever if I don't engage, go over. "Are you okay?"

Bianca, screaming, "NO, MOMMY, I HIT MY KNEE!"

Thank you, Captain Obvious. Now I'm slightly irritated. "Bianca, you can cry, but don't get to lash out."

"I'M SORRY, MY KNEE IS BLEEDING. I DON'T WANT TO DO MY REPORT NOW." (Let me assure you, it's about four drops of blood.)

"Take a deep breath."

Bianca continues on blubbering and attempting to talk at the same time, and I can understand none of it. Folks, this goes on for a full 15 minutes of straight-up Losing. Her. Mind. Then POOF, like a

magic show, she dries her tears, smiles, and is ready. I am in utter awe and check to see if her head is spinning.

She pulls herself together and sets up her "newsroom," complete with a desk (our standing desk TBG built), empowering coffee mugs (one with a picture of me in my 20s changing the oil in my car ((a gift from the parents)); the other with the quote "Here's to strong women. May we know them. May we be them. May we raise them."), computer and extra screen (for added effect). She gives an outstanding news report on Kate Middleton.

Amelia, complete with a bow tie, was the steadfast co-host for the first couple minutes, then opted to lay down for the rest of the report. No matter, the kid knocked it out of the park...even adding a tagline at the end, "This is Bianca Hoffmeyer and Amelia Hoffmeyer signing off." My journalist friends would be proud.

DAY 46
April 30, 2020

I'm probably one of the world's best procrastinators. My Mom always told me I worked best under pressure. So, I start making Bianca's cake at 7:00 last night and decorate it at 8:00 this morning. Yep, here I am winging it...again.

Let me be clear here. I am NOT a cake baker by any standard... but twice a year I roll up the sleeves and give it my best shot. It started when Brady was turning one; he loved everything trucks. I kept it simple and made a logging scene with heavy equipment matchbox vehicles, pretzel sticks, candy pumpkins and crushed chocolate cookies (dirt) on a big pan of brownies. I rocked it! It gave me the confidence to keep challenging myself, and since then, I have made a fish, a princess, Shopkins, a ghost train, a fire truck, a BeyBlade arena, Minions, Pokémon, a panda, a Transformer, and I'm sure a few more I've forgotten about. Most of them were decent; a few needed some serious help. When the fondant on the Minion ripped, the tears became scars; fangs and a cape were added and it became Count Franken-Minion. (So glad his birthday is close to Halloween.)

Whipping off cake-baking and decorating the day of the birthday without a solid game plan is not the recommended route. But hell's bells, here I am. I have two choices here: either pick colors and most likely pick the wrong ones and have to hear about it the rest of the year... or have her pick them. Yep, easy route.

As I'm trying to figure out left from right, Brady comes downstairs, and with full fanfare, announces the Birthday Queen, followed by her Royal Dogs. Down comes our strawberry blonde in a fancy dress, wafting around, with a crotchety old dog and klutzy puppy following along. (It's all about the entrance, you know).

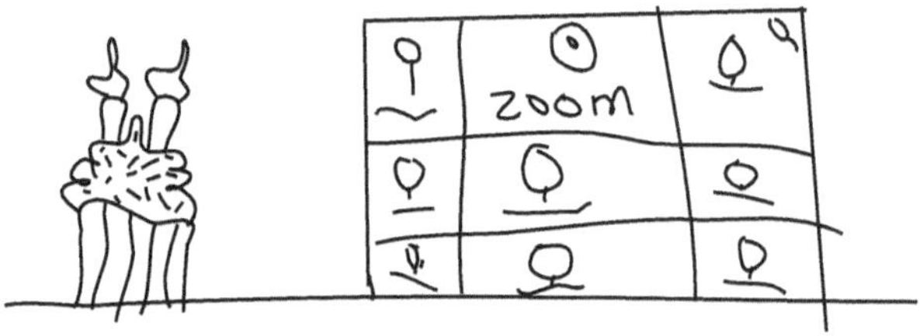

"Announcing Queen Bianca and dogs!"

"Hey Queen B, what colors do you want the cake?" (I'm guessing hot pink.)

"Green and Blue!"

"Green and blue it is." (Crisis #1 averted.)

I decide to make a jumbo cupcake with a woven basket pattern for the base in green buttercream. Have I done this before, you ask? Nope... but I'm YouTube-educated... it's all good. I rocked it out pretty well! I decide to put it in the fridge to let it solidify a bit. Sigh.. tragic move. One whole side slides against some random (and probably spoiled) leftover; and is messed up. Well, now it's going to be a solid green base.

Now for the top. Hmmmmm... decisions, decisions. (Yep, design-on-the-fly Hoffmeyer here). She wanted blue, but I figure I can do better than that! Another three different YouTube DIYs and I'm a pro. I'm going to do a multi-colored buttercream piping.

I somehow have to get three different colors in one piping bag. I piped them in rows beside each other on Saran Wrap, then rolled it, leaving a plastic wrap tail to fit into the piping bag and the tail is pulled through the piping nozzle. Ah yeah...that way-too-chipper chick on YouTube made it look much easier than it was. Thanks, Pollyanna.

I get my colors on the plastic wrap, start to roll it up, make a tail and do not have enough hands to keep it from oozing out as I get it into the piping bag. Sweet baby Jesus... I was a damn flight nurse and worked logistics in many abnormal situations in many foreign countries. Yet, I cannot figure out how the hell to get the unicorn frosting in the damn piping bag!

TBG comes over to help. He holds the piping bag while I carefully move the tricolor frosting into the bag and try to get the plastic tail through the piping nozzle. I think I would have better luck shooting darts drunk... in the dark. Frosting now pours out the side of the Saran Wrap... my head is about to explode. I'm wondering to myself, "Why do I put myself through this sadistic ritual twice a year?" I take the bag and whatever made it into the bag, and squeeze a little out. Well, I'll be damn...unicorn frosting.

I put swirls all over the top and the gap between the top and bottom layers. Masterpiece! Well, it was until I see the spots I missed.

Meh, that's what extra frosting is for. A little green frosting and voila, gaps filled. A few sparkly sprinkles later...and she's done! Another successful cake made for the year.

"Bianca, check it out," all proud of myself.

"Mommy, how did you do that!?!"

"I have my secrets." I'm feeling like the winner on Cupcake Wars, with a cake that looks like it came out of Nailed It.

The rest of the day was a whirlwind. Happy Birthday was sung by her classmates online. She was beaming. Then, on to gift opening with more online celebration. (Thank you to everyone who attended!) Friends stopping by with more gifts and giving lots of smiles and safe distance air hugs. In the background TBG and I are juggling meetings and school work with Brady. Needless to say, we are tongues on the ground by the end of the day.

The things we do to put a smile on our kids' faces. Worth every grin.

At the end of the day, I have a few minutes with Bianca. "How would you rate your day, with 10 being the best?" My inside, very tired, voice is saying, *You better be saying 11,000.*

"Hmmmm... a 9."

"What? Not a 10?"

"No, the icing on the cake was a little too sweet."

"I see," trying to hide my bruised ego.

Binaca, walking over and hugging me, "But since I got to spend it with my family, I'll give it a 10."

"Nice save, girl."

For all you new parents, soon-to-be-parents and not-parents-yet... here's a little advice. Never start a sentence with, "I would never...", because it will come back and bite you in the backside EVERY. TIME. Take it from the girl whose baking skill level is just above Nailed It and way below the Great British Baking Show, yet I gleefully pull out the mixer every six months with fantasies of smooth fondant and perfectly piped buttercream. Ahhh, to dream!

Let's pat ourselves on the back; we made it to another Friday! I know the world is starting to open up... but please be safe when getting out there.

DAY 47
May 1, 2020

We're taking a little break from life today to make a birthday video for our beloved Auntie Jen. Auntie Jen (aka Jennifer Chenevert), is my life-long best friend. We grew up in Colebrook, New Hampshire and have known each other since our first day of kindergarten. According to her, I came up to her and told her we were going to be friends. I'll believe her; I can't even remember what I had for breakfast this morning.

The kids have started to get into "themed" Happy Birthdays. They did an opera version for Oma; a *Star Wars* version for Uncle Benner; and "Youz Guyz" for Uncle Al and Cousin Edson. I'm curious what they are going to come up with this time.

"Hey guys, it's Auntie Jen's birthday today."

Bianca's eyes light up. "Ooooo, we need to make a special birthday song for her!"

"Mom, what is her favorite thing ever?", Brady asked.

Without hesitation, "Coffee."

They got right to it and proceeded to choreograph an entire coffee-themed Happy Birthday song for Auntie Jen within a half an hour.

"Mom, we need help from you and Dad. You have to turn the lights on and off for us."

"Um, okay."

The skit they did had them sleeping on the couch. The alarm goes off, light comes on, they pop up, grab their coffee mugs, cheer to each other, take a big sip, and proceed to sing "Happy Coffee Birthday To You!" It ends with them both going back to bed on the couch and the lights go out.

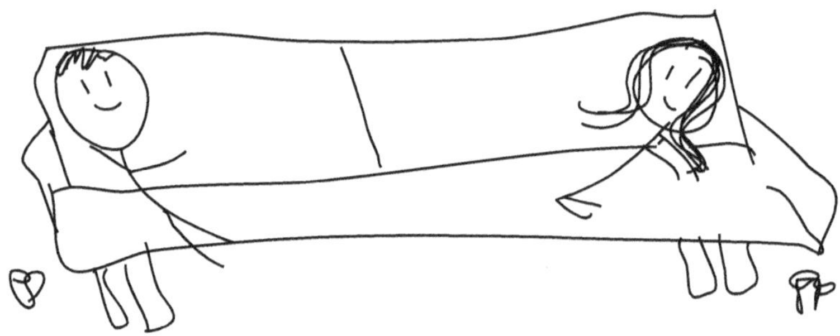

I was just impressed they could avoid fighting long enough to create such an awesome skit. Happy Birthday Auntie Jen!

DAY 48
May 2, 2020

OMG... can we go back to 8?

Today is Mommy versus a very sassy nine-year-old. Bianca is going through a deflection phase. When you try to have a discussion on something she is not interested in or you are asking her to do something she is not interested in doing, she will change the topic and act like she has no idea what you are talking about. Currently, she's trying to show me a picture, while I am asking her to pick up her shoes and socks.

"Bianca, pick up your socks and sneakers that are by the couch and put them in your bedroom, please."

Bianca twirls around the kitchen singing like it's time for her Broadway solo.

"Bianca, I asked you to put away your socks and shoes. If I ask again, there will be consequences."

"Oh, what? I didn't hear what you said. Hey, Mom, did you see my picture?"

Needless to say, it's extremely challenging and frustrating (like head-exploding frustrating)... and after more than a week of it, we're done.

"Bianca, I'm not looking at the picture until we're done chatting."

"See, see my picture," playing oblivious to what I just said and trying to stick the picture in my face.

Day 48

"We're done here. Technology is gone; you will remain in your room until it is cleaned and you are not coming out until you and I can have a discussion without the sass." Handled like a truly worn-out Mom. Well, that should take care of half the day.

Bianca mumbles under her breath.

I leave her to sit and stew a while. The one thing I know about this child is her dislike for social isolation. I'm pretty confident it will be less than an hour and she'll be ready to talk.

TBG is as frustrated as me. "Glad you're handling this. I'm ready to strangle her."

In the meantime, the eldest child comes up to me, all grins. Uh oh...

"Mom, you know those big ice packs that Dad put outside?"

"Yes."

"I opened them up and squished the stuff out. It looked like clear diarrhea!"

"Where did you empty it?" I am seriously afraid to know the answer.

"In the toilet!"

"Let's hope it doesn't have expandable properties when it hits water."

Thirty minutes later, Bianca roams downstairs. "Bianca, why are you out of your room?" I ask her.

"Just getting something."

"Sorry, back to your room."

Bianca sighs, rolls her eyes, and storms up the stairs. Five minutes after she goes upstairs I hear, "MOMMMYYY, I AM READY TO CHAT."

TBG is impressed. "Dang, you are goooood. Mommy 1, Bianca 0." I proudly stand in the champion pose. I roam up the stairs to finish up my conversation with her.

"Do you know why I want to talk?"

"My behavior and attitude," Bianca says matter-of-factly.

"Glad you know. You may not always see how you're behaving, and it's Daddy and my job to guide you back to the right track." At this point my Inside voice is screaming, *Holy crap. She's nine... what the hell are we going to do at 13?!*

"I'm sorry, Mommy." And she comes over and gives me a big hug.

And all's right with the world...at least for the next five minutes.

DAY 49
May 3, 2020

I think COVID19 fever set in on the Hoffmeyers today. We're all cranky. All except Lilo. She is a happy puppy, getting her belly rubbed by Brady. The simple things...

I figure we need to get out for some fresh air. "Let's go for a walk today."

One of the few times the kids are in unison: "I don't want to. Can we just stay home?"

"Oh, sorry, let me rephrase that: we're all going for a walk today."

The looks I'm receiving! I'm not even sure there's one emoji to capture all of it. I just ignore it. "C'mon, you can ride your bike or scooter."

Bianca, still trying to wheel and deal, "Can we do the little loop?" (It's 1/3 of a mile.)

TBG isn't having it. "No, we're going to do our usual walk, and since it's Sunday we'll probably go..."

I know where this is going. I totally cut him off to save him, not wanting to hear the whining. "We're just doing our neighborhood walk." I whisper to him, "Are you off your rocker? Tell her you want to do three miles and we'll have to hear it the whole way."

TBG just gives me an eye roll. It's okay, he knows I'm right.

Annddd this was the walk:

Bianca, three minutes into the walk, "I'm tired."

I'm not falling for it. "You need to walk to wake up."

Bianca, now five minutes into the walk, "Can you pull me on the scooter?"

"Nope."

Seven minutes into the walk. "It's hot and I'm tired, I want to go back."

Eight minutes: dragging behind.

Nine minutes: stopping to look at who knows what.

Ten minutes: "I'm thirsty."

Zero sympathy from Mom, "Keep up the complaining and we'll make the walk longer."

She wisely keeps quiet.

TBG isn't feeling it. "Well, isn't this the most unrelaxing walk? This is why we go in the morning when they're sleeping."

We made it through the walk... barely. The last half-mile, we let them race home. It was the nicest part of the walk. After the most unrelaxing walk, we figured we needed to air out a bit more and went for a ride. The kids both decide to bring their music and headphones. So now our relaxing ride turns into a shouting match between the two of them because neither would pull a freaking earbud out. Strike two.

TBG's looking like he's ready to run for the border. "So damn relaxing."

Well. tomorrow is Manic Monday... really hope today is not foreshadowing for tomorrow.

DAY 50
May 4, 2020

I'm exhausted. There's nothing more un-refreshing than a kiddo jumping in bed with you at 3 am. That was the end of it; it actually started hours ago.

10:00 pm: Bianca comes downstairs. "Mommy, I can't sleep."

"It's 10, girl... grab a drink of water and back to bed."

At midnight, TBG and I check on the kids before heading to bed. As I am kissing her goodnight, I notice she's smirking. "Bianca, what are you doing awake?"

Bianca, giggling, "I still can't sleep!"

"Turn on your music and get to bed."

3 am: The door squeaks open; I think I'm dreaming. Then I see an outline of a little body. Either this is a nightmare rendition of *Children of the Corn,* or my kiddo still can't sleep.

"Mommy, I can't sleep." I'm first relieved I'm going to live, and second annoyed I'm not getting sleep. I have two choices to make:

get out of my warm bed and go lay with her in her bed, or stay in my warm cozy bed.

"Jump in."

TBG just groans. Translation: "Crap, now *I'm* not getting any sleep."

Well, there goes my chance to sleep. Now Miss Sleeping Romper Room somehow manages to spread herself across the entire bed, while the two of us teeter on the edges.

6:30 am came about three minutes later. Mr. Don't Need an Alarm Clock pops out of bed and comes back 45 minutes later to drag me out of bed and walk the dogs.

9 am: We get back from our walk at 8:15 and I decide I'm going to run upstairs to do my 9 am meeting. Annddd then run back downstairs when I remember Sleeping Beauty is still in our bed. School can wait. I have zero interest in waking her and dealing with her grumpy arse.

10 am: TBG looks at me. "We need to wake her up... it's 10 already."

Brady interjects, "Dad, can you give it 30 more minutes? I like the quiet."

"I'm with him."

TBG, half-exasperated, half-understanding, "Fine."

10:30 am: A mini-zombie stumbles downstairs in a much better mood than I anticipated. To our surprise, she actually gets most of her work done in a couple hours.

2 pm: I'm trying to keep Bianca on track. "You need to get your reading done. Why don't you go out to the hammock and read?"

"Okay." She heads out with music and a book.

215 pm: I walk outside to check on her. There she is, completely asleep with her book laying on her.

That kid sleeps for three hours straight! She's sleeping so soundly, the dogs come over and lick her toes and she doesn't even move.

We ended the night celebrating birthdays! May is a busy month. Our nephew, Edson, is on the third and my brother Allen (a.k.a. Uncle Al) is on the 4th. The kids are loving customizing the Happy Birthday song for friends and family. Today they did a Bronx rendition they named "Youz Guyz" in honor of both Edson and Uncle Al.

I'm hoping there was enough activity going on to wear them out. I cannot do another *Children of the Corn* night.

Day 50

DAY 51
May 5, 2020

Random thought today. My 30s were A.W.E.S.O.M.E! I felt great, looked great, rested (for the most part), all body parts remained in the correct location...it was great.

I had the same expectations when my 40s came. However, this decade had a different agenda and it has been nothing but disappointment. This decade and I cannot seem to come to an agreement on the way to move forward.

My expectation is to keep wrinkles to a minimum, all body parts to stay in their relative original locations (without surgical assistance), hair looks like a mane, and energy equivalent to the Energizer Bunny. Not much to ask, right?

What I get is a forehead that could be mistaken for a Sharpe, body parts migrating across established borders, hair thinning where I'd like to keep it and growing where I don't want it, and the energy equivalent to Flash in *Zootopia* (Disney+, folks). Note to self: make sure the contract with the fifth decade is a little more specific.

But dammit, I'm still kicking it.

The kids are eerily good today. They get all their school work done by noon and are out playing most of the day. I'm sure they dodged something (c'mon, they're kids) or we're living in some parallel universe. No matter, they're outside and we get a little quiet. Nice to be able to think in complete sentences once in a while.

We decided we needed a celebration dinner for Cinco de Mayo. So pulled pork tostadas (flat tacos count for Taco Tues!) and margaritas it was. (Yes, yes... they were virgin for the kids; c'mon, we're not that bad!). For dessert, homemade Mexican chocolate cake. Now, you need to know I'm a sugar Nazi, so I made this with monk fruit, an alternative to sugar. I have always been some level of a health nut. It was exacerbated once we had a child who's sensitive to sugar. TBG didn't believe me at first. Then he picked up Brady from a field trip and the kiddo was literally vibrating from the excess of soda, ice cream, and cinnamon rolls. He was a convert from that day on.

Since it's the first time I've made this dessert, I needed to consult the critics. "Okay, how is the cake? Scale of 1-10."

Brady, talking as he's cramming it in his face, "Ten! Can I have more!?"

"Awww... thanks... no."

"Dang!"

TBG gives his approval: "Definitely a 10."

And then the harshest critic. Bianca, unimpressed, says, "Five."

I'm a little surprised. "Out of 10?"

"Yep!"

Of course, I'm a little butthurt. My sassy inside voice shoots back, *Little contrarian, last time I make you a cake!* However, the pseudo adult just asked, "Why?!"

"I wasn't impressed. I couldn't taste the cinnamon. It just tastes like chocolate cake. It's just not my favorite."

"I see." Now we're Nigella Lawson; awesome.

Brady was willing to assist. "Ooooh... I'll eat yours, Bianca!"

I decided to try a little reverse psychology. "Well, guess that leaves more for us."

"Guess so."

Well, so much for that.

DAY 52
May 6, 2020

I'll be honest...I've hidden out in the upstairs office most of the day. I'm trying to focus and actually complete a task. It hasn't done much good; the minions found me, and it's apparently 1,000 Questions Day.

Brady is my love bug. "Mom, can I have a hug?"

"Of course!"

"Thanks!", grabs a hug and runs off to play. I am seriously praying he stays this easy going through the teens.

I start getting into my work day, answering emails and responding to texts.

"Mommy, can I show you my book?" Bianca asks.

"Sure, baby." (Right as I'm in the middle of work text conversations.)

"So, this is Plinpix. Can I sit on your lap?"

"Sure." Now, here's me not at my finest. I'm mindlessly answering her questions to keep her chatting while I text. Here it is, parenting in the raw.

"Mommy, did you know...."

"Oh wow." (No idea.)

"Mommy, guess what?"

"What, baby?"

Yep, missed that comment.

"Oh, that is cool!" (So *not* winning it right now.)

"Mommy, now where did I leave off in my book?"

"I think it was next to the last page." (Wild guess.)

Yep, multitasking at its worst.

We take a break at lunch. I keep it short to finish what I hardly started. TBG is using it as nap time, and Bianca has crawled on top of him and snuggled. It's adorable for the moment.

Bianca decides to get up, isn't paying attention, and mistakenly sacks TBG. He curls up into the fetal position, moaning.

Bianca, looking confused, "Sorry, Daddy!"

I look over and realize what happened. "Bianca, you have to be careful when you get up."

"Daddy, did I hit you in the balls?"

TBG is now half-crying/half-laughing while holding himself. "Yes. It's okay. It's just an accident."

I am in tears laughing. "I'll be upstairs."

TBG shoots back, "Jerkface."

I continue to laugh as I hop up the stairs.

For the most part, the kids are actually really good today. They finish up their schoolwork and head out and play for a couple hours. I finally crawl downstairs and go outside to see what new adventure they've gotten into. I'm really amazed they haven't started a neighborhood social-distanced rave yet.

Bianca is out there with gloves; the neighbor kids all have masks on; Brady has a mask on and what I thought was blue gloves with the fingers cut out. Upon closer inspection, I realize he has taken blue painter's tape and taped up both his hands.

"Ummm, what is that?" I cautiously ask Brady, because I'm not entirely sure I want to know that answer.

"I didn't have any gloves."

"Brady, it's 90 degrees out! I'm pretty sure you're safe out here. You don't need gloves; you just need to wash your hands when you come in. Take off the mask before you hyperventilate."

"But I like my blue lobster claws!"

"I'd recommend taking them off before you get a free skin-removal treatment."

After dinner, Brady asks if he can have cake. Right behind him Bianca pipes up, "Can I have some too?"

Mom doesn't forget so fast. "Bianca, you said you didn't like it."

"No, I said it was a 5/10. It wasn't my favorite... but since it's the only dessert, I'll take it."

"Turd."

We let the kids stay up a little longer in an attempt to see the meteor shower. Lenny, Bianca's favorite stuffed animal, goes out watching in style, dressed in her doll clothes.

"Mommy, check Lenny out. She's ready to go watch the meteor shower!" She's showing me Lenny in a fashionable American Doll outfit, hat, and jacket. She's better dressed than I am most days of the week.

Day 52

Unfortunately, the Universe is not playing fair. The moon, way too bright, plus living in the suburbs equals a nearly washed-out sky.

I figured I might as well break the news to them, "I'm thinking we're not going to be able to see many meteors tonight." I look over, and realize they're not overly interested anyway, as they're cartwheeling down the sidewalk.

I'm getting Bianca settled for bed, and she wants to read for a few minutes. She pulls out her new US Atlas she used her birthday gift cards to buy. Zero idea where that came from, but way better than a Barbie in my book.

"Mom, my favorite state is Florida because they have oranges, their state bird is a mockingbird, and Auntie Ang lives there."

"Guess we'll have to visit." I didn't feel the need to mention all the tourist traps that are closed right now. Stupid COVID.

Bianca's eyes grow huge. "Mommy, did you know 425 Rhode Islands can fit into Alaska?"

"I do now."

"Mom, what is the state bird of New Hampshire?"

"Mosquito."

"Seriously Mom, no, it's a purple finch."

"Close enough."

"Mommy, did you know Vermont makes 100K gallons of maple syrup?" (I'm making that up...I forgot the number of gallons she said. It was a lot.)

"You know, New Hampshire makes it too."

"Yep, but not as much."

"But New Hampshire's is better quality."

"Really?"

"Really."

"How do you know that, Mommy?"

"Because I'm from New Hampshire." (For those that don't know, Vermont and New Hampshire have always had friendly discussions about whose syrup is better.)

"Oh…"

Not sure she 100% believed me, but she went along with it.

Day 52

DAY 54
May 8, 2020

I'm not even sure where the week went. It wasn't crazy, manic or chaotic... it just was. This is what happens when you live in blissful chaos on a daily basis. Calm is foreign and stressful.

When you're cooped up as a family in your house, surprises are a bit difficult. TBG went out and got a few groceries this morning. He uses these "grocery getaways" to take a ride and get a few minutes of solitude. We get groceries, he keeps his sanity for another day. I'd say it is a win-win. When he comes back, the kids go out to help him. They come back in hollering, "Mom, close your eyes!"

"Then how am I going to type?"

"You can type with your eyes closed!" Bianca shoots back.

"Good point."

When I open my eyes, there are two goofy, grinning kids holding bouquets of flowers squealing, "Happy Mother's Day!"

Brady chimes in, "They're too big to hide, so we're giving them to you now!"

"Awwww... thank you!" I'm soaking up the fact they're getting along more than they're giving me flowers.

On a whole different topic, Bianca's birthday gift from us was a hoverboard. I know, I know... you're probably hollering "hypocrite," as we told her she had to earn it. In our defense, we thought they cost $400; however, we found out they were much, much cheaper. So we opted to just buy it. The whole point was to show her how hard work, over a long period of time, will have a big payoff. However, we're in COVID times. Hot new toy, kids with cabin fever asking 1,000 questions/sec... yep, birthday gift it is!

This, of course, has a cascading effect. Specifically, one jealous brother. Between watching him look like a forlorn hound dog for a few days, and Bianca's 8,000 hoverboard rules she made up on the fly just to torture him, I mention he should count his tokens. Tokens, in our house, are pennies they earn to "buy" items. Kinda like they do with cigarettes in jail.

He lights up like Christmas lights and runs over to count his tokens. Well, wouldn't you know, he has enough to order his own hoverboard! He does a complete analysis of all hoverboards available on Amazon and settles on the same model as Bianca's in silver. We put the order in and find out it won't be coming in two days.

"Mom, how long will it be?"

"Well, it's giving an estimated date of three days."

"Ugghhhh.... seriously!?"

"Are you serious? You can't wait three days?"

"No, and it's just an estimate. That sucks."

After a torturous five-day wait (of which we were informed of every day past Day Three) his silver bullet arrives. Now we look like a modern version of the Jetsons.

Brady jumps on and is an immediate expert.. .at least in balancing on it. Controlling it is a whole other issue. I'm pretty sure all of us, including the animals, have track marks over our feet. Who even remotely thought this was an intelligent idea?

DAY 55
May 9, 2020

When I was stationed at Lakenheath, we had one of our techs hurt in a motor vehicle accident. Her mom, dad, and seven-year-old little sister were flown out to be with her. There were some days where it was more appropriate for the little sister to not be there. On those days, I would take her out to do fun things with her. One evening we went to the movies, and she was trying to run up the down escalator as we were leaving. Then she was flat out refusing to leave. I didn't have children then, and was trying my best to not make a scene... but in the end I had to sling her over my shoulder and carry her out and have the other person with me unlock her fingers from the chain-link fence as we walked by. I was heartbroken, because I knew she was acting out from all the chaos... and I was mortified at the scene I had made.

Scroll ahead 15 years... this girl has come a long way. If my kids hear the statement, "Do you want me to make a scene?", shenanigans instantly stop. Every. Time. They have never tested that limit, but know in their little hearts I would in a heartbeat.

Now, this is true in both discipline and defending my kiddos. This morning, Brady walks in the door crying. "What's going on, buddy?"

"Those boys are back and they were picking on me, calling me names, threw Nerf darts at me, and one of them pushed me. So I hit him across the side of his head."

Me and TBG just look at each other. Four boys have been coming down our street to go play at the basketball courts, and it seems like trouble is stirred up whenever they're around.

TBG darts out the front door, and Momma Bear follows. The boys take off down the road and I hear TBG holler, "That's right, run!"

Yes, folks, we're being *those* parents.

I look down the road and see them at the end of the street, and I holler at the top of my lungs "Stay out of our neighborhood!" and "If you can't play nice, stay home!" One of them stops and is apparently attempting a staring contest with me and waving. I happen to have my phone in my hand, so I act like I'm making a call. At this point, I'm pretty sure the neighbors are peeking out their windows... and I don't give a damn.

They take off around the corner and then peer back...persistent little buggers. Eventually they leave. Twenty minutes later, Bianca comes in, telling us they're on the basketball court again. Legal options are limited, so we do the next best thing: observe from our window facing the basketball court.

Brady asks if he can take Lilo for a walk. Now, this old girl wasn't born yesterday; Brady is a tweenie boy and he wants to test the waters. I tell him only around the loop we live on, and continue to do surveillance. TBG is doing the same thing from the backyard. The things we do when we become parents.

Sure enough, Brady comes around the bend and the four boys stop their game and perch on the side of the road. Awww, hell no...

I dart down the stairs and TBG already knows. "Yep, I see them." Brady walks by, and they're hollering something I can't make out. Brady comes to the house, lets Lilo off the leash a little too soon, and she darts over to the boys. Perfect timing...I walk over and get Lilo.

"Boys, I want to talk to you."

The boys are debating whether they have time to run

"I'm not going to yell, we need to talk," I calmly tell them.

They stop, and I'm sure pee is dribbling down a leg or two... but they listen.

Without getting into all the weeds, I told them the neighborhood is fun, my kids just want to play with them, and they're welcome here if they can behave.

One of the boys looks at me and said, "Ma'am, I just want to apologize." At this point I've brought our kiddos over, and all five boys apologize to each other and they all spend the next hour playing together.

I walk back over to the house smiling.

TBG looks at me, laughing. "Mom, the master negotiator."

"You know it."

This afternoon, Bianca comes flying in bawling. She just realized our neighbors were PCSing (moving) to Florida in about a month.

"Mommy, Anna is moving and she's my best friend!"

"Bianca, two weeks ago you said you weren't friends."

Bianca, sniffling, says through tears, "But she's changed, Mommy."

"Right, got it." (Please send wine.)

Brady decides he'll bring Lilo over to Bianca on the couch, to console her. He calls her over... and like a slow-motion scene, I see Lilo jump at the same time Brady springs forward and they collide heads mid-air. And now I have two bawling kids. Awesome.

Fifteen minutes later, I'm bending down to open the drawer below the oven at the exact moment TBG is coming up to the stove, and I take out his ankle. Lots of swear words and hopping around ensue. Life is getting back to our normal level of chaos.

At the end of the night, I tell the kids we have to do our push-ups. We're doing 22 pushups a day to raise awareness for veteran suicide. Bianca asks if she can do it by herself.

"Why by yourself?"

"You hurt your shoulder, and Brady has a headache."

"What about Dad?"

"Tomorrow... I got it tonight. And I'm going to challenge Ms. Johnny." (One of my close friends.)

"Well, okay... rock it out."

DAY 56
May 10, 2020

My Mother's Day starts out in perfect Hoffmeyer fashion.

7 am: There is nothing that can rip you out of a sound sleep faster than a dog getting ready to puke. Lilo is gagging away... I immediately spring out of bed, still unsure why I'm standing. Fortunately, we catch her before she lets it all go and get her outside.

8 am: I am gliding (probably looks more like stumbling, but I like to think of myself as graceful) down the stairs, waiting for my kiddos to attack me with hugs and kisses and have some creative breakfast made. What I get are two tweenies zoned out on the couch watching some cartoon, followed by a weak-sauce Happy Mother's Day after the big guy prompts them.

I look at them incredulously, "Seriously, you picked a cartoon over saying Happy Mother's Day to your Mom!?"

Brady jumps up from the couch and runs over to hug me. "Sorry, Mom...Happy Mother's Day!

Bianca, sauntering over, "Happy Mother's Day!" and proceeds to kiss me on the cheek and gives me a pat on the head. Nothing like feeling like a pet.

9-11 am: Brady is squirreling everywhere but on his task. Aggrrrhhhh, the joys of ADHD. He has chosen to join the yearbook next year as one of his electives, and had to submit an application to be accepted. He hasn't mastered typing yet, so he either hunts and pecks or uses voice to text. I'm explaining he needs to practice typing, because it will help him in the long run. The child hates handwriting. I take solace in reminding myself handwriting and intelligence are not directly related. (I'm a nurse and have had to decipher many doctor's orders.)

We somehow get on the "When I was a kid..." conversation, and we're explaining the difference between a typewriter and word processor—two terms he has zero concept of. He's mind-blown to think we had to use corrective tape, and that we typed directly onto paper.

We get back on track. He has to discuss why he would be a good fit for the yearbook staff.

"I have a good trait—I'm an extrovert."

"Good one. I would consider myself an extrovert-introvert. I like to meet and help people, but I also like my alone time to decompress and recharge."

"Everyone has a little introvert in them, Mom."

Well damn, that was profound. "You're right, kiddo."

2 pm: Even though the day started off a little wonky, it turned out to be a great day. We went to the Circuit of the Americas on the very east side of Austin and got to drive our car on the racetrack in exchange for a food or monetary donation. It was awesome seeing all the people who showed up in vehicles ranging from beaters and minivans to classics and exotics. The one thing that was the same... everyone was smiling and waving to each other. It was one of the

first times we took the kids out for any adventure since COVID started. The only downside was being restricted to 20 mph. While we understand why, TBG was DYING to open up his M3. It really was the ultimate test of restraint for him. No matter, it was a once-in-a-lifetime experience, and it was pretty amazing. Best Mother's Day gift... glad I thought of it.

We get home and decide to take the kids out for a little ice cream. When we get back, I meet a friend at our house to look at a few houses. I thought it would be easier for her to drive and me to navigate, "Why don't I jump in with you and we can go?"

"Okay."

We proceed to jump into what I thought was her vehicle.

She looks at me. "Fancy. You're going to have me drive?" The comment didn't register in my little brain, as I thought she was talking to herself. She's trying to start the keyless remote starter. "It's saying there's no key in the car."

So I ask the obvious question: "Where did you leave the keys?"

"Donna, this isn't even my car!"

The car we hopped into belonged to a friend of the neighbors across the street. I assumed it was my friend's vehicle.

Plus, the vehicle was unlocked.. and I assumed she unlocked it.

Oh crap, I thought you got a new vehicle!" After we stopped hysterically laughing, we got in her massive truck parked behind the car we were in and went on our way house hunting."

After we drove around the neighborhood, unsuccessful and bummed we didn't have any prospects, we turned the corner to my street and Bianca's words rang in my mind: "Anna is moving!"

"I think I found your house!"

"Wait, what?" My friend is completely confused.

"Wait here just for a minute."

"Um, okay." She's looking at me, wondering if I need help.

Once I explain to our neighbors that my friend is looking for a place in this neighborhood to be closer to family, and she's interested in their house, they let her in immediately. One hour later, they have their house sold. Dang, I'm good... I think I need to start charging commissions when I make these connections.

DAY 57
May 11, 2020

Attempting to teach delayed gratitude to our children in this day of technology and Amazon feels like walking backward on a slick treadmill set at a 45-degree angle.

I mentioned a few days back, Bianca received a hover board for her birthday and Brady had earned enough tokens to also get one. A mere five days later it's on our doorstep. That seems pretty quick to me. However, not to our dear son; you would have thought he was having a fingernail pulled out each those five days.

"Alexa, do we have any deliveries today?"

"No deliveries today."

"Alexa, when is my hoverboard going to be delivered?"

"The hoverboard will be delivered on May 14th."

"OMG, that's three days away! Why does it take so long?!"

I couldn't resist. "Pretty sure she isn't advanced enough to answer philosophical questions, kiddo."

"Mom, stop."

Bianca has become a fan of the Atlas... World Atlas, US Atlas, history of the Atlas... Atlas, Atlas, Atlas.

"Mommy, can you look up the cost of this atlas?"

"Baby, it's a fourth edition... you already have the fifth edition."

"Right, I'll get all the editions."

"No, that's not how it works. The newest edition has the previous edition's information, plus the newest data."

"Oooohhhhhh. Okay, but there is another one I want."

"Do you have enough tokens?"

"Yes!"

We ordered a Road Trip and a World Atlas. I'm thinking she's all set to plan our next vacation! Sweet!!!

Six seconds later....

"Mommy, when are the books coming in?"

"One tomorrow and one a couple days later."

"Dang, it takes a while."

"Dang?! Girl, life has been a bit too good to you. You can wait."

"But I really want to read them."

"Trust me, they will still be readable a few days from now."

I look at the order tonight, and they'll both be here tomorrow.

We obviously have some work to do on immediate gratification and patience.

DAY 58
May 12, 2020

Okay, so my plan was to start writing earlier tonight, and I was on track until I was derailed by a pretty emotional nine-year-old.

I mentioned before that her good friend Anna is moving to Florida; casualty of a military lifestyle. She's having a hell of a time coping with it for reasons I wasn't expecting.

"Mommy, Anna is my really good friend."

"I know. It'll be tough, kiddo."

"Yeah, and I don't hang out with the other girls in the neighborhood because they're all trying to wear makeup, text, and act like teens!"

I'm half-sad and half-proud at her statement. "Bianca, you have to understand that in the next coming years there are lots of hormones and changes that will be occurring with all of you. So have grace with your friends... you won't do it right all the time either."

I have now decided if I'm going to survive motherhood, I need a subscription to a wine club. I'm seriously considering starting a GoFundme.

Her friend leaving and feeling alone was the crux of the problem. But to get there, we had to take the long route through multiple topics.

Bianca explaining her sassiness: "See, my eyes and nose and mouth try to stay straight and listen. But my brain says *Noooo* and I start acting silly. So, I just need a new brain."

Bianca, explaining why she has difficulty listening and turning off the sass: "It's like a figure eight. See, if you leave a little opening, I can shut it off. Buutttt... if I close that loop by mistake, it keeps going and going and I can't shut it off."

Bianca, explaining her anxiety with growing up: "There are people that kill and hurt other people in this world... they are bad. If I ruled the world I could squish all of them...but since I don't, they'll still be out there to deal with." Seems like a fair assessment.

Bianca's take about growing up too fast: "Mom, some of my friends are trying to look all pretty and act weird when boys are around. I don't get it. I just want to play with them... get all dirty playing... why can't we just do that?" (Yep, Mom's peacock feathers are showing.)

Of course, this conversation takes place at bedtime. An hour later, she is now feeling cathartic, happy, and ready to sleep. I'm completely drained, wondering why Day Drinking for Moms of Girls has not become an Olympic sport yet.

After all is said and done, she's got her head on straight. It's just going to be a huge lesson on learning to stand on her own.

DAY 59
May 13, 2020

For the last week or so, our lovely daughter has been quite challenging. (That's putting it nicely.) Most likely she's taking in all this chaotic energy and struggling to process it. Between the pandemic, remote learning, and her friend leaving, it's definitely causing a disruption. There's also no doubt she has inherited a few of my genes: stubbornness, standing her ground (even when it's obviously crumbling under her), "witty humor" (some people call that sassy), and having no issues telling it like it is. Yep, all my best traits packaged up in a beautiful, smart, lovable girl. I know this child is going to go places. Now, whether that's going to be a CEO or the head of a gang is what is in question. God bless her future partner.

Fortunately, as with life, she goes through cycles. After a few intense discussions with her, I am happy to say attitude is back in check, sass is at a manageable level, and listening is up 80%. All is right with the world again... for now.

Today there's only one focus for me: get this dang shoulder taken care of. About a month ago, I missed a step coming downstairs. Unfortunately, my hand was on the railing, and when I missed the step, my hand remained on the rail, driving my shoulder up and forward. Amazingly, it only hurt for a sec and I thought I was good to go the next day... and I was. It was three weeks later when I started feeling like the Tin Man.

I'm a nurse; it comes with unique character traits. So I do what any awesome nurse would do. I ignore the pain. It only hurts in certain positions; therefore, I just avoid them. Makes sense, right?! Meds... nah. Rehab... I'm putting away dishes, that counts. Besides the kids impulsively tackling me and nearly ripping my arm out of the socket, I'm doing pretty good.

TBG just shakes his head. "You know, you'd be up my back end about seeing the doctor. Make the call."

"Giving advice and taking advice are two different things."

"Make. The. Call."

I know if I don't, he will continue to razz me. I make an

appointment with my doc. And in COVID fashion, the first appointment will be a telehealth appointment.

My doc is pretty awesome. We're laughing as she's trying to have me move in certain positions to get an idea on what's going on. Here I am, in my kitchen, with a phone to my ear, making odd motions with my right arm...and occasionally yelling "Hell no!" when it hurts too much. If anyone walks in, they might consider committing me.

She decides I need X-rays and an injection. I need to go in... which leads me to today.

I have one meeting before my appointment. The beauty of telework meetings is that you can keep the video and mic off (connection issues, of course) and do whatever you damn well please. So, as we're in this meeting, multitasking Mom is getting dressed, brushing my hair, and getting a little makeup on before I dart out the door for my medical appointment. Uh-huh...I got this. (Well sorta... I *am* still a minute late.)

After my X-ray, I meet with my doc. Looks like I have inflammation and possibly an impingement. Needle time! But before we get there, she has to know exactly where to put it. "Relax, and I'm going to move your arm. I want to see if you still have range of motion regardless of the pain."

Regardless of the pain?! That does not have a good sound to it.

At that moment, she takes my arm and moves it UP. OVER. MY. HEAD! Holy Batman Balls! I wasn't sure if I was going to cry, throat-punch her, or both. Dammit, she could at least offer a shot (alcohol, not needle kind) first.

Now, I'm not afraid of needles per se, but I know when it's smart to look the other way... this is one of those times. I know exactly how long that damn needle is; I also know I don't get topical anesthetic, just a needle straight into my shoulder space. Yep, looking away is just smart business.

Chichuwowa! If you have never experienced this sadistic pleasure, I don't recommend adding it to your bucket list. Sweet 6.5-pound Baby Jesus, I feel like my shoulder is going to explode with all the pressure! For that moment, I'm extremely grateful for all the meditation I've done in the past. I'm getting lightheaded... phew... and a bit nauseated. No, I'm not a drama queen. I'm sucking it up. She has no idea I'm 30 seconds from passing out. Fortunately, I reach nirvana (the place, not the band) before I pass out. The pain immensely dissipates. I can raise my arm to shoulder level without pain. I'll try above my head in a few minutes. Baby steps here...

Yep, I'd do it again.

I get home and the kids are enjoying the day. I'm thinking to myself, *It's 80 with intermittent rain and a balmy breezy 70 this evening; my Northeast friends are dealing with random snow showers, and I'm not missing any of it.*

Brady comes running in, "Mom/Dad, Sam and I are playing this game where we race down the hill on our skateboards and try to make the other one fall." He's proudly showing me his scraped knee and butt cheek.

Me and TBG look at each other and wonder where we went wrong.

I am Mom, therefore forced to give a public service announcement. "Ummm, I'm glad you're having fun, but socks, shoes, and a helmet are a must."

"Awww, Moooommmmm."

"Awww nothing." I am not budging. This Mom-Nurse is not interested in an ER visit during a pandemic.

TBG and I, like the rock-star parents we are, take advantage of our medical experiences and tell him every TBI (traumatic brain injury) case we took care of over the years, and all the residual damage and issues they had.

That does the trick.

After picking his jaw up and putting his eyeballs back in his head, he goes outside and puts on his helmet, shoes and socks... no questions asked. HA! Parents 1, Kid 0.

DAY 60
May 14, 2020

School is definitely winding down. The workload is lighter, and the kids are getting their work done at warp speed. Somehow that memo didn't make it to our work; we seem to be speeding up as they wind down.

Fortunately, they're pretty good about keeping themselves entertained. Sometimes, they get pretty creative.

Brady and his friend Sam created a skateboard racing game. We've already gone through the wearing helmet and TBI horror stories and he's wearing his helmet faithfully. Now, the shoes are a whole other battle. Our kids love to be barefoot as much as possible. For the most part, we let them go for it. I figure if their feet start melting on the 190-degree Texas pavement, they'll get off it. However, when it comes to using their bikes, scooters, skateboards, ripsticks, etc, the rule is socks and shoes. Yet somehow those articles of clothing miraculously fall off as they get on their toys.

Over the last 5 years, TBG and I have repeated the same message over and over and over: "Put your socks and shoes on! You're going to thank us when you fall and your toes aren't chewed up."

The kids always respond the same: "Yep!"

And 30 seconds later, after any lecture we've given, "Mom/Dad I'm bleeding... I hurt my foot/toes/ankle."

And we have the same response, "Where are your socks and shoes!!!??? How many times do we have to go through this?"

Apparently many, as the cycle continues; only they keep upping the ante. Now Brady is getting his adrenaline rush with this skateboard game, and he has road rash on his thigh, knee and now ankle.

"Mom, my ankle hurts!"

TBG is quick to respond, "Bet if you wore socks and shoes you wouldn't be complaining."

I give the standard nurse response, "It's just a little road rash. Wash it and put a little Neosporin on it. And maybe try some socks."

"I can't wear socks... it's raw."

TBG looks at him in awe. "But it wouldn't have been if you wore socks and shoes!"

"Dad! Stop it!"

"Just saying."

Brady goes into self-care mode. "Mom, can I take a bath?"

"Okay, but do not put cinnamon and peppermint oil in your bath this time!" He loaded his bath yesterday with cinnamon and peppermint essential oils... he looked like he got a mild sunburn. He's lucky he didn't burn his skin off!

I'm retiring just in time for so many reasons. Obviously, the first one is to protect these kids from themselves. Second, the afterschool program at the Youth Center cut their availability in half, so we would either have to leave them home alone or find alternate care. I could only imagine the mischievous things they would come up with if left to their own devices.

I am counting my blessings. Life is working out the way it needs to; the kids are healthy (banged up, but alive) and I made it to the end of another week, mostly intact.

If you made it too, give yourself a pat on the back. If you made it without day drinking... well, I'm not sure if that's good or bad. Either way, congrats!

Day 60

DAY 61
May 15, 2020

TBG and I have some advice for anyone considering marriage and children: DO NOT PICK MAY TO GET MARRIED.

Now, we were originally planning on a September wedding, but a few things put a wrinkle in our plans, the biggest being that my time in the military was extended nine months because of a glitch in the system. The military offers tuition assistance, but it comes at a price. For every class paid for by tuition assistance, so many months are added to time owed in the military. Let me just add here, I was the one who realized there was a glitch; I was the one who told the appropriate entity; and I was the one that caused myself to be extended for nine more months. Sigh... the price for honesty is steep sometimes. Little did I know we were actually saved a lot of potential problems. It was a destination wedding on a cruise ship... in September (September 11th, to be specific)—smack dab in the middle of what turned out to be one of the most active hurricane seasons ever. So, with the Universe's help, we moved it to May.

Here's the problem with May (at least in the warmer parts of the US): school finishes at the end of May. That means all the end-of-year wrap-up occurs throughout May. We end up inundated with school plays, last-minute projects, desk emptying, signing up for school next year, an emotional roller coaster because friends are moving (welcome to military life), etc. It is a hot mess time of year.

And forget a babysitter; they're all busy with the same. If they're college students, they're graduating or finding/starting summer jobs or taking a breather and filling up their social calendar.

We have one more flavor to add to the mix: TBG's job. He usually has to go out of town 5-6 times per year, and fortunately has a bit of flexibility in his schedule. So he will often adjust around holidays, birthdays, events, and the start and stop of school. We have always agreed it's easier to sacrifice our anniversary and celebrate on another day so he can make events and end-of-school for the kids. So, for the last fourteen years, between deployments and TDYs (going out of town for work), I can count on one hand the number of anniversaries we've celebrated on the correct day. This year was one of them.

COVID, of course, has thrown a wrench into our usual style. Since we've decided we're not quite yet ready to venture out with the reopening, we ordered pick-up from a local restaurant. If you like wood-oven cooking, Kindling Texas Kitchen is the place to go!

Of course, the garbage disposal we identify as our son wants in. "Can I get something too?" our tweenie asks.

"Sure, what would you like?" Like we have any option at this point. Either we get him food, or he comes around asking to taste-test.

"Salmon!"

Leave it to our kid to find nearly, if not, the most expensive entree on the menu. He's going to have such a rude awakening when he has to start affording his own groceries. He'll be going from home cooking and fine dining to take-out, clearance aisle deals, and crackers under the couch cushion. The wee one/fussy eater isn't going to be left out and decides on the cornbread appetizer... hey, corn is a veggie!

The majority of the day is one of us on a telecon adding to the to-do list, while the kids finish their little bits of schoolwork and go out and play. (Which, I would like to add, doesn't include the skateboard road-rash game. Brady said all his road rashes hurt too much.) And somehow, we ended up with a tent in the front yard.

Brady is running to the freezer, grabbing ice packs. I'm looking for bumps, bruises, bleeding, or a combination of the three. "What are you doing?"

"Making a homemade air conditioner for the tent. Ice packs and a fan!"

I'm half impressed and half visualizing ice pack guts all over the yard.

"Okay... please return them."

"I will."

"Famous last words." (Yes, they were right where I predicted: left in the front lawn for Brian to chew up with the lawnmower.)

We have our "fancy" dinner, complete with wine (my favorite part of the meal) and decide the rest of our "date" will be a just-released movie with the kids, *Scoob*.

Don't ask me how it was; I fell dead asleep on the couch. TBG debated on letting me just sleep there (no, it wasn't the wine, I only had a glass), but figured I'd rather be in our bed (he was right). Annndddd after a few hours of sleep in the bed, we had the company of a nine-year-old woken by and scared of a storm... and TBG takes it all in stride.

To this, I give a big shout-out to TBG. Happy Anniversary, Babe! You are my superhero, rock, handyman, best friend/husband. Thank you for laughing with me at all our blissful chaos!

DAY 62
May 16, 2020

I find kid dynamics interesting. One minute they're best friends, the next, bitter enemies. Emotions are on the surface and raw, no matter if it's a hug or tears, an apology or verbal barbs, it's all done with full-on passion. Excitement overrules delayed gratification. They can be a total mess one minute and giggling and laughing the next. Their emotional freedom is curious, refreshing and challenging (emphasis on *challenging*).

The other day, Brady wouldn't let Bianca in his room because he wanted some quiet time. Bianca was upset so she went to his board and adjusted his "good morning" sign to "poo head." (Admit it, you giggled). After he let her back in, she went and changed it back. He righted the wrong in her eyes, so she would do the same.

TBG was managing the home front today, while I went out to help a dear friend move into her beautiful new home. Six hours later, I return to an exasperated husband. Apparently, one of the kids in the neighborhood was a bit eager to play with our kiddos. We'll just call him B for simplicity.

10 am (Door knock). It's B.

"Can the kids come out and play?"

"They're cleaning their room. They'll be out in an hour."

"Okay."

10:05 am (Door knock). And it's B.

"Are the kids done cleaning?"

"Not yet, B."

"Okay."

10:10 am (Doorbell). Yes, you guessed it... B.

"Are they almost done?"

"Buddy, when they come outside, *then* they will be ready to play."

10:15 am: TBG sees that B has crawled behind the bushes and is looking in our window to see if they're done.

10:20 (Door knock). Our friendly little B is back. TBG is now meditating and practicing mindfulness to avoid any unduly sarcastic comments.

"Are they done yet?"

"No, not yet. When they come out, they'll be able to play."

"Well, what are they cleaning?"

"Go play and they'll be out." TBG is kinder than me. My comment would have been something along the lines of, "If you keep coming and asking, you'll get to find out."

At the same time, our two have the attention span of a gnat, and weren't getting their room cleaned. At 11, TBG decides to give them (and him) a break to go play... in hopes they could come back in a few hours and finish up. He brings them back inside at 1:00 PM.

1:05 pm (Door knock). The one and only B.

"Can they come back out?"

TBG is now sending up prayers to keep his cool. "Not now, they're finishing cleaning their room."

"Okay."

1:15 pm: TBG goes outside and B's bike is in our driveway and half the garage is pulled out into the driveway...and there's B, riding down the road on the kids' scooter.

TBG calls him back to come pick up his bike and gently asks him to put the scooter back. "When the kids come back out, you can use the toys."

The kids finally get back outside around 2 pm... and now TBG is dealing with Brady making sleepover arrangements with our neighbor's son without talking to the parents first. God bless this child.

"I told Sam everyone (he's one of six children) is coming over to watch a movie and then Sam and the girls were all going to sleep over our house."

Poor Sam, who wanted a sleepover with just Brady, got mad. He just wanted a little of his time without his 4 sisters. Who could blame him?

TBG looks at Brady quizzically. "Why are you making decisions without asking the parents first?"

"I thought that was the plan?!"

TBG takes a deep breath. "Brady, no. Mom, I, and Sam's parents will get it organized. I know you're trying to help... but right now, don't."

"Fine."

At the end of the day it all works itself out. Maybe at the expense of wearing Dad out, but it works out.

DAY 63
May 17, 2020

I feel today is the perfect day to get a few projects done and maybe even, dare I say it... relax.

The kids are playing and, amazingly, helping TBG outdoors. (Let's all pause for a moment of silence.) I'm taking advantage of the quiet. I make some pretzel bread, practice my flute, and fold a little laundry. I even find time to swing in the hammock and read. It may have turned into reading behind my eyes for an hour or so. This NEVER happens... and by never I mean N.E.V.E.R. I'm pretty sure the model of children we have comes with a "parents-are-having-quiet-time" detector, and like a magnet, they come swarming us. I'm trying hard to enjoy the peace versus bracing for the cacophony of "Hey Mom! Where are you? I need..."

Hell, I think *The Sound of Music* was even playing in the background.

And then dinner comes along, and we're back to reality.

Just before dinner, I'm messing around on Brady's hoverboard. It's pretty easy to use, but does have a few glitches... like when it goes from one surface to another. I was trying to ride it over to plug it in, and in the process ran over the dog's tail and lurched forward... causing me to jerk forward and my arms to fly backwards to counterbalance. Holy Mama... I feel a searing pain from my neck to my right bicep. Did I mention I hurt my shoulder coming down the stairs a few months ago? I don't recommend riding a hoverboard when you're injured.

TBG sees my face contort. "Seriously, Donna..."

"It only hurt for 10 seconds, tops." (We'll worry about residual pain later.)

During dinner, TBG is looking out the window at the dogs. Amelia is chewing on something. I'm now looking at Amelia. "I think she's chewing on a stick."

"Ummm, nope... she has a bird."

We all just look at each other.

TBG and the kids run outside, and Amelia is snacking on a bird that our cat Puck took down. There's only one small problem... it isn't dead.

TBG takes a shovel and throws the bird over the fence.

Bianca walks in crying. "Mommy, the bird was still alive!"

"Come here. baby." (Giving her a hug.) "The bird was dead. It was just the last bit of electrical energy making the body move." (I'm thinking on the fly here... don't judge.)

Bianca is now sobbing. "Mommy, the head was moving and eyes were blinking!"

"It's okay...it was just the rest of the bird's energy." I'm sticking to my story.

"But, I don't want the bird to die. I like birds! Why did Puck do that?"

"Baby, it's his instincts."

"Well take it out of him!"

Brady, attempting to be helpful, chimes in, "Bianca, it was only the wing that broke."

"Brady! How about we just end the conversation?"

"What?" Brady is looking at me confused.

After I take him aside and explain that the whole "dogs eating a semi-live bird" is a bit traumatizing for her, he connects the dots. "Ohhhhhhhh...."

Ahhhh... out of the mouth of babes. I know he'll get it one day. Just not today.

DAY 64
May 18, 2020

I'm stressing a little. The end of school is a mere three days away. We're finally in a rhythm; the kids are conditioned like Pavlov's dogs, and now we're heading into uncharted waters... telework and summer vacation. How in God's name is this supposed to work?

Schedule! We got this. This will be brilliant. Video and TV time will be bought with chores. This will keep them busy, out of most trouble (let's be realistic, now), teach valuable lessons, and the house gets cleaned! It's the ultimate win-win!

Today reinforces this need for a schedule. I go outside this afternoon to check on the kids. TBG comes out and calls Brady over.

"Brady, what did I tell you about using the spray paint?"

Ahhhh... that's where the paint smell was coming from!

Brady looks sheepishly to TBG, "To ask..."

"Yes, buddy... you keep using up the paint I bought for projects." TBG is looking at a broomstick handle Brady decorated for his ninja role-playing.

TBG follows the trail of spray paint through the grass and around the corner of the house. Bianca quickly pipes up and decides honesty is the best policy. "Daddy, we used the glow-in-the-dark and painted a smiley face on the side of the house."

"What!?"

"Sorry. Daddy, we were just playing."

It's gonna be a longggg summer.

Of course, we have to go look when it gets dark. Right now it doesn't show...but it might not have received enough sun yet. Stay tuned.

Ahhh, yes... definitely need a summer schedule.

DAY 65
May 19, 2020

Like I said yesterday, it's gonna be a lonnnngggg summer.

Our homeowners association has decided they're going to keep the pool closed for the summer because they don't have a lifeguard monitoring social distancing. Oh, COVID, you strike again.

Let's just say the neighborhood is not wildly happy about this. Those of us with extremely active kiddos are even less happy.

I bet a day with our two little darlings would change their mind. Yes, yes... I'm all about precautions, but I'm all about sanity too. There is a sweet spot between the two... somewhere. Many-now working-from-home parents without childcare are desperately trying to figure out that balance. It's definitely an ugly dance.

Ahh, and speaking of kiddos... they lucked out. Their spray-the-side-of-the-house-with-glow-in-the-dark-paint project didn't pan out. They didn't spray the side of the house heavy enough for it to glow at night. Sorry to disappoint y'all.

Today is Show and Tell, webchat style. Bianca is so excited to show off her dogs. They, on the other hand, are not as excited. Bianca is begging Amelia to come with her and she is just sitting at my feet. Lilo is just spinning in circles, all excited because that's what puppies do. "Bianca, go get a carrot and Amelia will follow you." Amelia is an equal opportunity gorger, from meat to veggies to fruit.

Carrots and apples are a favorite. Lilo is too, only because Amelia taught her.

"Okay, here Amelia!" she calls to them, dangling a carrot in front of her, immediately getting her undivided attention.

Bianca gets them all situated and now she can't get onto the meeting. Poor kid is so bummed.... stupid technology. However, we're a step ahead. We take a picture and submit it to her teacher. BAM... adapt and overcome, girl!

There are two days left until the school year ends and summer officially starts. All ideas to entertain two very active, adventurous, semi-mischievous, keep-you-on-your-toes kids are needed. Google, help!

DAY 66
May 20, 2020

The day starts out a little rough for Brady, but ends on a good note (and lesson learned).

Brady is checking his Google classroom for any last-minute updates from his teachers. "Oh no... the list came out for Yearbook. I wasn't picked."

He had to pick an elective for 7th grade. It was between Yearbook or Computer Technology/Spanish (a semester of each). Brady took Spanish in elementary school and came out of six years of Spanish knowing "*hola*" (no reflection on the teacher... he just wasn't interested). I think Brady would choose milking venomous snakes over Spanish (sorry, Tia). Needless to say, Yearbook was his save, or so he thought.

When he selected Yearbook, he thought it was a matter of just signing up versus being selected.

Brady was pretty upset, "Mom, now I have to take Technology and Spanish! I don't want to take that."

"Well, sometimes life throws you curveballs. Maybe if you take the technology course it will give you more skills and a better chance for the Yearbook next year."

"Hmmm... maybe. Still don't want to take Spanish."

"Maybe you could ask him if he could give you advice on how to improve your chances to be selected next year... and maybe let him know you would be interested in a fall-out spot."

"Okay! What's the worst he could say?"

Brady sent the teacher an email, and that afternoon he had a response from the teacher. His eyes lit up. "Mom! Mr. Miller is letting me join Yearbook!"

Apparently, Mr. Miller was so impressed with the fact he took the time to respond and ask for advice to improve that he was willing to bring him on the staff. (Mom may or may not have peeked at his email before him... hush... no judgment).

Let's hope that is a lesson that sticks with him. And yes, I rock.

Mom: 24,358,334,964 Kid: 1 (I'm sure he's been right on something *one* time).

TBG taught Brady another lesson today.

We were sitting on the couch and our eldest dog, Amelia, unapologetically climbed on the couch and pushed her way to her spot. When you are 13½ in dog years, you have your "spots." In the process she stepped right on Brady.

"Ouch! She stepped on my balls, put her butt in my face, and didn't even apologize!" howled Brady as he doubled over on the couch.

"It's only the beginning, buddy," TBG empathetically told him.

"Awesome," Brady whimpered.

DAY 67
May 21, 2020

This morning started off with a bang. I get a migraine about once a month and can usually break it with Excedrin and a caffeinated drink. I'm that weird non-coffee/soda chick. If you see me with something with caffeine in it, it's most likely for medicinal purposes. The downside is that a cup of coffee taken any later than 9 am will keep me up for hours.

So I didn't crawl into bed until 2:30... am.

I slept through what I thought was my alarm. When I did wake up (at 10 am), my phone rang three minutes later and a friend called to chat. Brian walked up the stairs saying the guy would be here in 30 minutes.

What guy?

I also have a missed call and a text from another girlfriend asking if I'm okay because she got a call from our alarm company. What?!

Here's the story. I *did* sleep through my alarm, as well as a phone call from the alarm company. No idea what alarm went off to alert the alarm company.

In the meantime, TBG had taken the dogs to the groomers. Brady called to tell him the alarm was going off (yes, I slept right through it) and he told him how to shut it off—but not before the police stopped by to check on things.

Brady answered the door and said his Mom was sleeping and Dad was out. Apparently, that was a sufficient answer. (That surprised me a bit.) Brian gets home and wakes me up 30 minutes before the contractor comes out to give us a renovation estimate... which I have completely forgotten about.

To top it all off, I don't find out the entire alarm story until after the contractor leaves. Once I hear the story, I am confused why Brady didn't come get me.

"Brady, why didn't you wake me up?"

"You were sleeping, Mom, and you had a headache."

"As much as I appreciate that, sweetheart, this would be a time to wake me."

"I'm sorry, I didn't want to bother you."

Can't get this child to stay out of my face when I'm in the middle of a conversation, baking, concentrating on a project, or on the phone... but house alarms are going off and police are stopping over and he doesn't want to bother me. Bless. His. Heart.

Well, school is officially out today and we are now the proud parents of a 4th and 7th grader. It was underwhelming and unceremonious, but they didn't care. They were just relieved to be out from under parents pseudo-teaching them and pseudo-parenting them. Now they get us as full-time pseudo-parents. COVID forced the Youth Center to drastically reduce their availability for the summer to essential personnel only. Yeah, with me retiring in 4 months... I am definitely not on the essential list.

So we get to entertain two kids for 3 months while we are both teleworking. Awesome...

It's gonna be an interesting summer.

DAY 68
May 22, 2020

Yesterday was our school-is-over-and-we-need-to-put-closure-on-this-hot-mess-of-a-year party.

Now, please understand, I am not a party planner of any sorts. Ask any of my friends that have witnessed my skills. If you plan it at a cool bar, you don't need to decorate; drinks with friends take care of the rest. Since we're dealing with our children, those are not an option (oh, and that whole COVID thing wipes out any other thoughts of a parent-survived-school after-party). Soooo... we're going to keep it simple. Pizza party and Nerf wars!

Two large pizzas + eight kids + Nerf arsenal = Smiles

TBG has become the resident Nerf modification expert. He modified one of Brady's blasters, and Brady gave it to his friend Sam. Now the playing field is leveled. And like any 12-year-old boys, they find ways to crank up the excitement.

Bianca comes running over, "Mom, I don't want to play outside anymore."

"What's up?"

"Those Nerfs hurt!", lifting her shirt, showing me mini-welts.

"How close are you?"

"Close enough to get these." Bianca accidentally got in the line of fire. Brady and Sam were actually intentionally shooting each other at close range... because it was fun.

Needless to say, there were some rules of engagement revisited.

"Boys, we need to revise the Nerf War rules."

"Huh?"

"You guys cannot shoot each other at point-blank."

"What's point-blank mean?" Brady asked.

"Close range."

"Oh. But it's fun!"

"It's not fun when someone is caught between the two of you. Your sister has little welts on her."

"Well, tell her not to get in the middle then."

"Brady...."

"Fine."

"At least 10 feet apart. We don't need any ER visits, especially right now." That's my warning for doing anything where there is even a remote chance of an ER visit.

Day 1 of summer break, and only a minor injury. Not too bad.

DAY 70
May 24, 2020
(The 23rd was amazingly unremarkable)

There is nothing like waking up to, "Mom, can I go to the lake with Sam? Dad said ask you."

As I'm attempting to peel an eye open, I mumble "Huh? Whatever Dad said goes."

Needless to say, he was a bit bummed, because I already knew Dad's answer was Hell No. We knew everyone and their brother would be at Canyon Lake, splashing and playing. We have to also figure in the Brady Factor. His impulse gets the best of him, and he'll be all over people in no time at all. We're not quite there yet.

Fortunately, there were plenty of kids around to distract them. Unfortunately, they were all boys. Bianca saunters over to me. "Mommy, that boy Jack is very nice."

I'm bracing myself for the next statement.

She continued, "He let me be his ammo person during Nerf Wars. The other boys said, 'Oh that's your girlfriend.' and he said 'No, she's my friend.'"

"I like Jack."

"Me too," Bianca says with dreamy eyes. Oh Lordy...I'm not ready for any of this.

I started singing "Oh Mickey" (If you remember this song... you're old) and replaced it with Jack's name.

"What song is that, Mom?"

"Oh, Alexaaaa… play Mickey."

This leads to a karaoke session of *Mickey* and every other one-hit wonder of the 80s and 90s in the kitchen... complete with a dance-off.

TBG walks in and wonders if I have officially lost it.

Bianca looks over at him, "Dad, I like your voice better."

I start singing louder and dancing around her nonstop.

"Mom, stop."

TBG smirks, "Good luck with that, Bianca."

As I'm dancing and singing loudly, I laugh to myself and think, *The teen years are going to be SO. MUCH. FUN!*

DAY 71
May 25, 2020

Today is Memorial Day. Although there are always circus antics going on in our house, I just want to stop and give focus to the day. After almost 21 years of service, I've seen more than my share of loss. When this day comes around, I often reflect on many situations I've encountered either directly or indirectly and the people we have lost on this chaotic journey:

USS Cole Bombing

Twin Towers Bombing

C130 plane crash in Afghanistan

Kabul shooting

Brain tumor

Aneurysm

Suicide x 4

Motor vehicle accident x 3

...on top of the patients lost.

Some of these I was directly involved in, others I was support for family, and sometimes I was both. Every single time there was a level of grieving and reflection.

Sometimes I'm surprised I continue to have a positive outlook with all these events. I guess if anything, I'm grateful. On April 27th, three days before our daughter was born, there was a shooting in Kabul that killed nine U.S. military service members TBG was deployed with. If TBG had not been sent home two weeks early from his deployment, he would have been one of the victims. Bianca's early arrival saved his life.

So, no matter what day you're reading this collection of stories, please take a moment and reflect on what you are most grateful for in this life.

DAY 72
May 26, 2020

The last couple of nights have been a bit harrowing on the weather front. Here's the breakdown:

Sunday:

We have a tornado warning. Now, let this northern New Hampshire native give her perspective. The San Antonio weather folks absolutely *suck* at reporting tornadoes. We lived in Little Rock prior to moving here, and they could tell you where the tornado was to nearly the second. My first close call was in Little Rock. TBG and I were in our office working, and Brady was upstairs in his crib sleeping. All of a sudden, I started hearing this weird siren noise.

"What is that noise? Is that the Klaxon thingy going off?"

My husband, who never panics, very directly said to me, "Turn on the TV, now." And low and behold, we had a tornado watch, with a tornado heading *right toward us*. The weatherman was giving a minute-by-minute rundown on where the tornado was heading and who specifically needed to immediately shelter. It was the most accurate weather reporting I had ever witnessed.

Let me remind you that, up to that point, I had never even remotely experienced a tornado. Needless to say, I was very nervous with a 5-month-old baby, puppy, and really no safe place to take shelter. The house was built in 1963, and the only place without windows was the hallway... *if* we closed all the particle-board doors. I figured the only thing we had going for us was that the house was originally from 1963. If it had withstood that many tornado seasons, it must be some level of safe (or just lucky).

So, there I was on a futon mattress we put in the hallway, with a baby and a puppy. TBG was standing in the front doorway looking at the sky, while on the phone with his Dad (in Michigan).

"Donna, come here for a second."

"Are you crazy?! Get out of the doorway!"

"It's okay, come here." He had been listening to the weatherman and giving his Dad a play-by-play on the phone. His dad was a weather junky and fascinated with tornadoes. TBG knew it wasn't going to directly hit us, but it was way too close for my comfort.

I have no idea why I listened, but I crept over and looked outside. The sky was green, and it was eerily calm.

"Listen," he said to me.

And there it was... the faint, but growing, freight-train noise. I'm pretty sure I felt a few drops of pee run down my leg. The funnel cloud was about a quarter-mile to the left of us. As it passed, I could feel the rumbling in my chest. The funnel didn't touch down until it was about a half-mile down the road.

I say all this because we (okay, at the time TBG) had 1000% confidence in the reporting. And over the next couple of years, those weather folks saved a lot of lives because of their accuracy.

Here in San Antonio, we had a tornado bend a water tower near a friend's house about two miles from us, and neither of us received a tornado warning! Compared to the Little Rock crew, our reporters in San Antonio are the drunk dudes in the bar playing darts blindfolded.

Let's add the fact Bianca has a *bit* of anxiety when it comes to bad weather.

The last tornado warning we had, Bianca screamed, "We're all going to die!" while the four of us plus two dogs were crammed in a teeny bathroom.

Day 72

Needless to say, it puts us a little on edge when we hear tornado warnings. However, this time she did much better at keeping calm... probably because we didn't put her in the bathroom.

Brady decides to bring down his entire bedroom ...just in case.

Monday Night:

Heavy thunderstorms, no tornadoes.

Bianca wakes up and comes downstairs. "Mommy are we going to die?" After our friend's house burned to the ground from a freak lightning strike, she's convinced we're going to experience the same fate.

TBG gently says to her, "Bianca, I'll go upstairs and lay down with you."

"No thank you. I'm going to stay here. I think I have less of a chance of dying downstairs."

TBG and I just look at each other.

I try another angle. "Do you want to go lay down in Brady's room?"

"He's in your bedroom, Mom."

"*Sigh*, lovely." In the midst of trying to settle Bianca, Brady somehow made his way to our bedroom and became a fixture in the middle of our bed.

TBG encourages her, "C'mon Bianca, Daddy will go lay down with you." He knows his fate is sealed.

I walk into our bedroom, and there's 86 pounds of boy... and this girl ain't moving him. I think I might be able to wake him enough to walk him back to his room. Yeah, WHATEVA!

So now TBG is sleeping with one minion and I'm sleeping with the other one. Fun times.

This morning, TBG and I both look like something ran us over forward and gleefully reversed over us. TBG looks over at me. "How did you sleep?" He probably knows the answer just by looking at me.

"I didn't. He kept trying to sleep sideways, and got angry every time I tried to have him move over. You?"

"Every time I moved, she would either put a hand or leg on me."

So happy we have good weather today...

DAY 74
May 28, 2020
(Either the 27th was uneventful, or I am now losing time.)

TBG is in his glory. One of his favorite things is to be outside doing yard work. Today he was laying compost and sod in the backyard. Brady was a trooper and worked with him the whole time. Bianca gave it a go and lasted a couple of hours.

She came in and, like a little magnet, found her way to where I was working.

"Mommy, can I color my Barbie's hair?"

"Sure." We have powder hair color, and I figure that's a relatively safe project to keep her occupied. Yeah, that lasted for about 5 minutes.

"Mommy, can I cut my Barbie's hair?"

"Well, my concern is it doesn't grow back, and you may regret it."

"I promise I'm only cutting it a little."

"Okay, but I don't want to hear it.... and do *not* get Barbie hair everywhere."

It ends up a slightly crooked bob, but she does pretty well. Way better than I could have done.

When I walk in our bathroom, I noticed my makeup had been messed with. Specifically, my bronzer looks like someone took a backhoe through it.

Bianca, did you play with my makeup?"

No, Mommy."

"Bianca, you lied to me the other day and have to earn our trust back. I hope you're sure about this."

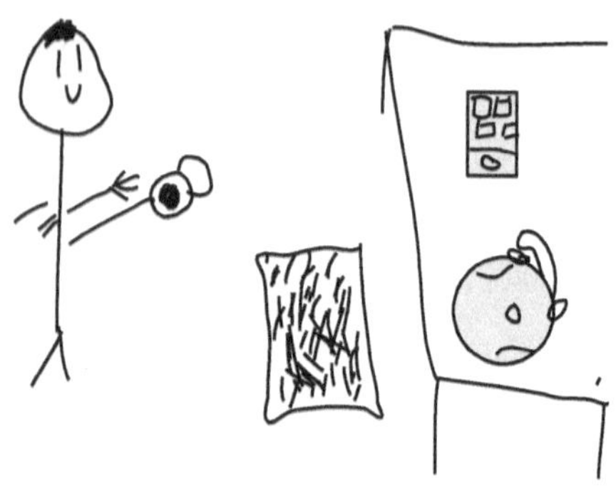

Mommy, I didn't touch anything."

Later that evening, we're putting the kids to bed and all talking in Brady's room.

"Brady, did you play with my makeup?"

"Well, see, we were watching *Ant-Man*, and he was lifting fingerprints to break into things. So I tried using your bronzer to see if I could lift your fingerprints and try to unlock your phone."

Me and TBG just look at each other and then him, and say in unison, "WTH!"

"Yeah, it didn't work."

It's going to be a long summer…

DAY 75
May 29, 2020

Mom crashed last night... it was a never-ending week.

I am not organized by nature. If you could crawl in my brain, you would have to duck, bob, and weave to dodge all the squirrely thoughts zooming around. So to compensate, I have to have checklists, to-dos, calendars, and schedules everywhere. Which leads me to dread school letting out. (Crazy, I know.)

At least with assignments, they were kept busy the majority of the day and we knew where they were. With school out and their "creative" little minds, I have visions of neighborhood raves, "science" experiments, and just pure madness. (Okay, might be a little dramatic...but you get the point.)

I queue Google for summer schedules for kids and the "Did You Do This, Then You May Do That" schedule popped up. This consists of cleaning rooms, cleaning bodies, chores, reading a book at or above their reading level, typing, and practicing music. Once that is completed they can go outside, have an hour of video, and 30 minutes of TV. Brilliant!

I'll say overall, it's working... but the crafty ones are learning the faster they get it done, the more of the day they have. So by the end of the week, they're done by 10 am, which most likely translates to pencil-whipping it. Looks like we'll be starting with inspections.

"Do you understand the difference between quality and quantity?" I ask them.

"Nope!" in unison.

"Quality is how well something is done. Quantity is how much is done."

Blank stares. Nothing is registering. I continue, "So in regards to chores, when you are going faster, you are not doing it as well. I'm not saying it has to take forever, but taking five minutes isn't producing a good product either. Bottom line, faster is not better. I'll be checking behind you."

"Mooommmm... it's summer!" both moan.

"Yep, and you two can clean up after your tornado-selves." They know they're not going to win the argument, so they both concede. Wise choice, kids.

Yesterday was a beautiful day. The wee ones spent the day outside playing with friends. Apparently, it was dress-up day. Bianca walks into my office in a flight suit (she's determined to be a fighter pilot... look out, world). By the time I take a break in the afternoon, she's dressed as a she-devil. Considering the meltdown she had earlier, I almost ask if there's a poltergeist costume in the mix.

I walk outside to check on them, and it looks like there was a theater massacre. They took their dress-up boxes and brought them outside and the whole neighborhood is pretty much playing dress-up. There are shoes, shirts, pants, scarves, necklaces, and sunglasses strewn from our yard to the neighbor's.

Bianca gets big kudos for cleaning it ALL up and putting it all away, while her brother plays in the backyard... he is really owing her today.

When she had her meltdown (details are irrelevant, they all have the same start, middle and end... and you've already heard it a few times) she needed a few

minutes to cool down. Brady went outside, and her friends asked where she was. Sir Blabbermouth proceeded to tell them she was in trouble with Mom and why... to which the little girls proceed to call Bianca over, when she does come out, and say "Brady said blah blah blah." Which sends her right back in the house crying because she's embarrassed.

"Brady, what in God's name were you thinking?"

"What!? I was just saying..."

I cut him off before he can finish: "There's the problem."

Oh, but wait, he makes sure he outdoes himself. That afternoon when the kids are out back playing on the trampoline, Brady decides to be Mr. Cool and tell his friends her nickname is "Ms. Poopypants" (a nickname we gave her before she was potty-trained). Of course, the boys all start calling her that and she comes back crying. Fortunately, she has a resilient side and we tell her if she blows it off it, will blow over.

I look at our eldest, stunned. "Brady, are you kidding me?!"

"Sorry, Mom, I only told Hudson and told him not to say anything... and he did!" (All shocked and mad because he's getting in trouble again).

"Are you serious? Would you like us to whisper our family nickname for you when you were a baby?" (Mr. Peepants.)

"No!!!"

TBG is as stunned as I am. "I rarely say this, Brady... but that was stupid."

And yet after throwing her under the bus, twice, she cleans up everything outside. She asks to sleep in his room tonight. He gives her a resounding "No."

"Brady, I need you to think twice about that answer, after the shenanigans you pulled today," I warn him.

After a little back and forth (and Mom slightly pressuring the guilt) he gives in. Seriously, child, after today you owe that girl whatever she wants.

The funny part of it is that it's usually Little Miss pulling stunts like this. Looks like Brady has a bit more spice in him as he gets older. And the adventure continues...

DAY 76
May 30, 2020

TBG is determined to have our backyard completely covered in grass. He chooses to ignore the fact we live in southern Texas. He has killed weeds, fertilized, seeded, reseeded, overseeded, watered, and prayed for years. It has come a long way, but there are still areas that just refuse to fill in. He finally broke down and sodded the patches.

And like clockwork, dogs are peeing, kids are jumping, cartwheeling and rolling... all on his new grass. TBG is crying (man-crying = swearing), "Forty-eight freaking hours, that's all I want."

"I know, honey, but you know in our house plants and animals have to be resilient to survive."

"Grrrrr..." he mumbles as he walks off.

Bianca asked if we could play the game Beat the Parents. The name pretty much explains the game....kids against parents ask each other questions and move their piece a space for each right answer. First team to the finish line wins. Sounds simple enough.

Parents: "What is the name of the garden Adam and Eve were in?"

Kids: "The Enchanted Forest."

Parents: "Ummm, close-ish...but nope. Garden of Eden."

Kids: "That's not close!"

Parents: "We were being nice."

Kids: "In what sport is a 'stalefish'?"

Parents: "Cricket?"

Kids (laughing uncontrollably), "No, snowboarding!"

Parents: "People from America are called Americans. People from Denmark are called what?"

Kids: "Denmarkians." (Seemed like the obvious answer to me).

Parents: "No, Danes. What is the pronoun in this sentence. 'She had a cell phone.'"

Bianca: "Cell phone!" (Ummm...we may need to revisit sentence structure.)

Brady, looking exasperated: "She."

Parents grinning, "Too late..."

They kicked our butt, mostly because the game ended quicker if we lost than if we tried to win. (Don't judge... y'all been there.)

DAY 77
May 31, 2020

Summer has started!

The kids have been in heaven, sleeping in and spending their days playing outside with friends (after their Mean Mom To-Do list is complete, of course). I love watching them drag out their dress-up clothes, makeup games, share ice pops with the neighborhood, and have their greatest worry be who got the better Pokémon card.

I've said it a couple times, but we work hard at limiting the amount of crap they have to hear about the outside world. They're well aware of COVID; we're on them every day about wearing masks, keeping six feet from friends, washing doorknobs, countertops, and hands. Hearing about the infection rate, death rate, people's views, and personal tragedy stories is just too much, and robs them of their innocence. I fiercely try to protect that innocence.

But there comes a point where you can't hide them from all the ugly. Currently, it is the protest resulting from the death of George Floyd. They have to understand: even though the world is often unfair, it doesn't mean you don't stand for what is right.

Today we sat our kids down and explained the protests and why they are occurring. We explained how as parents of white children, we don't have to worry about certain things parents of black children do. We explained some of those differences and how it is an unfortunate and unacceptable reality.

We explained how the police are protectors, but like any group of people, there are bad seeds.

Bianca is trying to process all this information. "Why would he do that?"

"I don't know, kiddo. Just remember, most police are good. Mr. Tony is *not* like that."

Bianca, wide-eyed: "He would never do that!"

We explain that protesting is a way to take a stand and show the people/government that what has occurred is not acceptable, and a change is required.

We explained the difference between protesters and looters, and why the latter is using a peaceful event for their personal, self-centered agenda, causing people to lose focus on the reason for the protest.

I went on to explain how a dear friend of mine's daughter and son coordinated a peaceful protest in Eugene, OR today. I told my wee ones the strength of Maddie and Spencer; how they were erroneously blamed for destruction that was done by looters the night before their scheduled protest, yet they kept moving forward and had one of the few successful peaceful protests in the US.

Bianca looked at me with those big green eyes. "Mommy, wasn't she afraid to still have the protest?"

"I'm sure she was, but she's a very strong person. It didn't matter what anyone said. She knew she had nothing to do with the people who chose to loot. They both chose to keep moving forward and rocked it out."

Bianca was in awe. "Mommy, I need to meet her!"

"Maybe one day you will."

It was not a conversation we wanted to have, but one we needed to have. But at that moment, I knew they understood and could handle more than I realized (or wanted to believe). It was a little bittersweet; a bit of innocence was lost... but it was so worth the awareness.

DAY 79
June 2, 2020
(Definitely losing time. No idea where June 1 went)

Life got a little zany the last couple days. I am in the final months of my military career. I have two months until I go on terminal leave (using up saved vacation days for all my civilian friends), and four months until I officially retire, which really has not been a forefront thought. COVID has caused enough of a distraction that it hasn't really clicked, until recently, that my days are numbered and I am really retiring... unless the military opts to not let me go. (Oh, yes—when we sign the dotted line, we give up more than most realize.) With the surge that was occurring in places such as NYC and not having a clear vision of the need for medical personnel, there was a chance (although pretty slim) they could have retained all medical people leaving the military if they felt they needed the bodies.

So, with that uncertainty, with COVID throwing us into telework and limiting resources, my attempt at winding down seems futile. If anything, I feel like I have more work at warp speed.

Juggling work and kids out of school... sweet Baby Jesus... the chaos knows no bounds! The neighborhood has sprung up children from every corner of the Earth and they've adopted our house (outside) as a good spot for a home base. Don't get me wrong, I love having them over...they're good kids. However, when you're in a meeting with kids hollering requests for help and food and you're trying to focus on the meeting while simultaneously listening to see if any of the hollers are life-threatening...well, it gets a bit insane.

Bianca comes running upstairs, "Mom, the boys' mom is here and wants to meet you."

Two of the boys in the neighborhood have started coming over, and their mom had stopped in to meet us, which I appreciate immensely. Of course, at this very moment I'm in a meeting, looking

like a hot mess with my wild hair, glasses, and old T-shirt and workout pants.

"Okay, be right down!"

Zero time to look in a mirror; social distancing will keep any body odor from wafting her way. Glad I still remember to brush my teeth. Sorry, lady... this is the best I got.

I mute my phone, zoom downstairs, and out the door, praying no one in my meeting is going to ask me a question in the next 10 min.

"Hi! I'm Donna," I say cheerfully, hoping it will make up a little for the mess she's looking at.

"I'm Mandy... just wanted to come over and meet you and make sure it's okay for the boys to be here." (Of course, she looks impeccable.)

"No problem. They're fine here playing outside with the other kids. Apologies, I'm in a meeting right now (holding my phone up) and kind of look like a hot mess."

"No worries... we live just two roads over. Yours are welcome to come over."

She's very nice, and I'm glad she stopped in. At the same time, I'm trying to subtly listen to my meeting while we talk, just in case my name is called. I have no doubt I looked like an idiot trying to discreetly eavesdrop.

Really, really glad retirement is getting close. At the pace I'm going, I'll look like I either need a makeover, to be committed... or maybe both.

DAY 80
June 3, 2020

It's just been one of those days of randomness.

Our neighbor behind us had a very old and very crooked tree. I loved that tree, so it's bittersweet to see it cut down. On one hand, it was running into our peach tree and causing it to bend; on the other hand, it was so beautiful, and I always enjoyed watching squirrels and birds scurry around on it. The nurse in me felt I had to watch the tree trimmers cut it down, so I could say, "At the time of the incident..." (warped nurse's mind... sorry). My Dad is a logger, so I am very familiar with safe practice. This did not resemble it at all. I was convinced there was part of the house or fence coming with it. But hells bells, they landed it perfect. Our peach tree is forever thankful.

TBG works with planes in his current job. Bianca has determined she wants to be a fighter pilot. So when Dad announces to her that he had a plane brought into town to fly a few sorties, her eyes light up. Being the cool Dad, he offered to bring her to check out the plane. I thought she was going to pass out at the offer. Sitting in the plane is definitely a bucket list item for her. I'm not sure which one is more excited.

The pets are in rare form today.

Lilo is on a crapping/peeing/puking inside the house streak... specifically the kids' room, and more often than not Bianca's room. Lilo seems to have an affinity for pooping beside her bed. Apparently

I'm the one to blame for this. I get wrapped up in work, and she lays beside me all day. Instead of walking downstairs and asking for the door, she enters stealth mode, roams into one of their bedrooms and takes care of business. Sigh...

Our cat, Puck, is a butthole. He keeps randomly attacking people. We started letting him out during the day and all was well, until it wasn't. He was at the neighbor's in a bush and took a swipe at him. They couldn't go out their door without him getting all feisty...and it was only at their house. Puck never went to anyone else's house. Needless to say, he lost that freedom and is stuck in the house (like we need another child). Now we have a depressed cat. Seriously depressed. He sits on the back of the couch looking at us with mopey eyes, hoping we'll give in and reduce his sentence. Sorry, Puck, be a butt and pay the price.

DAY 81
June 4, 2020

If I start the morning late, then typically I don't get back on track. That was me this morning. I slept through my alarm and woke up to a call from a co-worker. (Nothing like trying to sound awake when you have no idea where you are.) I blame this all on COVID. Teleworking has caused us to lose all sense of calendar time. Medical providers can no longer accurately assess if someone is oriented, because none of us have any idea what day it is anymore.

The rest of the day didn't get any better.

TBG comes around the corner, "I'm going to take the dogs for a walk."

"K... just let me finish this phone call and I'll go with you."

TBG gives me the "seriously?" look. "Ummm...you have a 9:15 meeting." (It was 9:06.)

I had completely blanked out. "I do?" (20 seconds later) "Oh, right I do!" Stupid COVID, now I can't even remember meetings. Give me another month and I'll just be staring out a window with a little drool coming out the side of my mouth.

Since we have no idea how long we're going to be stuck in these four walls, we decided it was the perfect time to start renovations. Currently, we're in the midst of getting quotes. Let me tell you, after getting a few quotes, you start building confidence in your DIY skills. Our evenings are now spent watching YouTube DIY projects and saying, "Yeah, we could do that." (Pretty sure people feel they could do any of those projects when it's videoed in fast motion.)

On a good note, we found a person who fits our budget, and in a few months Pandemic Parodies will become Horrors of Home Reno.

Let's hope that's just a funny name.

Right now, the states are struggling with how to reopen businesses but still keep people safe. I totally understand how difficult it is to balance the economy and health. I do not envy local and state governments right now (or ever, for that matter). My view, for our little family of four, is to sit back for a month while they attempt to reopen and assess the situation.

This does not make the choice easy when you have two very active kids. Trust me when I say I really want life back to normal, just like every other person. However, I know we still have to keep precautions. We are hand-washing, gel-rubbing, daily-shower-taking fools... plus, we wipe down every package that comes in the door. If there's no major spike in two weeks, then I think we'll be good. But it's far from perfect. Like everyone, we're trying to balance between physical and mental health. It's like a teeter-totter with the big kid jumping on and off.

Bianca comes flying down the stairs. "Can I go to Eve's house?"

TBG doesn't even flinch when he responds, "No."

"But Mom said maybe!" Ah, the peg-the-parent-against-parent game. Often attempted, never works.

"I wasn't there for your discussion. You need to talk to her," TBG quickly responds.

"Mooom, can I go to Eve's house?"

Okay, I'll spare the dialog. There was a bit of back and forth between us. I finally asked TBG to come upstairs to shut down this Mom vs. Dad game she is trying to incite.

"I didn't know Dad said no, Bianca."

"But you said maybe."

"I'm sorry, I support Dad," I say, thinking this will be the end of it. Yeah, spoke too soon.

TBG speaks up, "I'll tell you what..."

Oops... he made the fatal Dad mistake. He looked into his daughter's puppy-dog eyes... invisible rays that melt the heart.

He continued, "You can go to her house for an hour. But! You have to wash your hands before you go, and shower when you come back. AND, if you bargain, it will not happen again."

Bianca's no fool. "Deal!" She washed her hands and ran like the wind before anyone changed their mind.

I looked at TBG, shaking my head, smirking, "Sucker!"

"Shut it." He walks off, knowing he got owned by a strawberry-blonde, green-eyed little girl.

We're all trying our best, folks... give grace.

DAY 83
June 6, 2020
(Wait, was there a 5th?)

Phew. Sometimes this world catches the best of you, and you're just holding on for the ride.

Right now there's a lot going on... wrapping up work (which seems to be unwrapping as fast as I can wrap it), trying to out-process (basically clearing a bunch of checklists to be allowed to retire), Mom duties, and trying to breathe in the midst of all the chaos. Honestly, I've given up on breathing; I'll do that after I retire.

But it's also summertime, and we gotta let kids be kids as much as possible. Our neighbors and their six kids are moving soon, so they have been getting their last bits of fun time in. We decide to let Brady's friend Seth sleep over. This was not an off-the-cuff choice. We know their kids are locked down as much as ours, and it gives a teeny sense of normalcy to them.

"Mom, we're going to do the All Night Challenge!" Brady says, all excited.

"What exactly is the All Night Challenge?" I have a pretty good idea, but want to make sure it doesn't include any questionable activity.

"We just stay up all night and play video games, read, and play card games. That type of stuff."

"Uh huh. Do you think you can actually make it all night?"

"Yeah!"

"You better not raid the refrigerator."

"Oooo... good idea. I mean, nooooo we won't do that," Brady says, giggling.

Wouldn't you know it, they made it until 7 am! Seth looked way better than Brady. Brady looked like a Mack truck hit him. However, he managed to make it all day and didn't fully crash until 10 pm tonight. We may not see him until tomorrow evening.

It's interesting to see the various ways children respond to stress. It amazes me how they can pick up on nonverbal cues.

Bianca's responses when she is around her friends are, like many kids, less than desirable. "Bianca, it's five... can all of you pick up before you leave to go over to the girls' house?" I ask her. Each of the girls immediately starts picking up... except one little diva.

"Bianca, let's go!"

Bianca decides it's time to try on an old tap outfit, sing *The Sound of Music*, and admire herself in the bathroom. The other two girls have cleaned over half the room by this point. Needless to say, there are a few unpleasant conversations between her and Mom, a few tears, and hopefully a little reflection. Ahhh. Learning is fun

DAY 85
June 8, 2020
(I'm sure there was a 7th; it just slipped past me.)

It is definitely a Monday. Forgot to charge my phone last night, which means no alarm and slightly oversleeping. This is one of the many reasons telework rocks; my commute distance is 10 steps. Let's see, what else? Oh yes, Brady broke a glass, the bathtub has a leak... yep. definitely Monday.

On a whole other note, I have decided we are either rocking out this parenting gig and totally empowering our kids, or completely screwing it up and they're ready to jump ship.

Bianca comes running over all excited, "Mommy, Daddy helped me design my house!"

"Where's the house for your parents?

"I can put a Granny-flat in the back."

"Granny-flat??"

TBG starts laughing.

I'm curious to find out her grand plan. "Where are you going to live?"

"Minnesota."

"Seriously? You're from southern Texas, can you handle all that cold?"

She's looking at me like I'm a nutball, "Duh! That is why I had a fireplace built... so we could sit there and the kids could have hot chocolate."

"Gotcha. How many kids are you having?"

"Four. Two boys, two girls."

"This mom is not a fan of the cold, girl. I lived in it for 18 years."

"You and Daddy will fly in from your tropical Hawaiian place and probably only stay a week because it's too cold."

"That is a real possibility, girl. Are you going to work?"

Giving me another "Duh" look, "Ummm, yeah Mom, I'm going to be a pilot, remember?"

"Hope your husband can handle all the kids. What will he be like?"

"Weird, kind, and handsome... and not dorky weird, just a little weird."

And there you have it. Bianca has her life planned out. Hope her future husband is ready.

I figure I'm on a roll. Might as well see what the other one's future plans are.

"Hey Brady, what are your plans?"

"Dunno."

"How many kiddos are you having?"

"Dunno."

"You're right on track, kiddo."

Apparently, Bianca was also trying to right her wrongs before she became a parent and confessed a bit more on "Showergate". (This is when our darling children were faking taking showers by sticking their head under the faucet.)

I was complimenting her on her hair-washing skills. "Dang, Bianca, when you wash and condition your hair well, it feels and looks like silk."

"So, Mom, when we were faking taking our showers..."

Crap, there's more? "Yes...?"

"We would turn on the shower, wet our hair in the sink, put wet footprints on the bath mat, wet our arms down, and clean up the sink area." (Now smiling, all proud of herself.)

"And where did that get you?"

"Ummm... nowhere."

"Right. Now you get Mom and Dad checking behind you. I think it would have been easier to just take the shower."

Bianca is now looking a little sheepish, but I can tell she's still quite proud of herself. I realize we have either a future CIA/FBI agent or cat burglar here.

EPILOGUE
(Day 86 and beyond)

At this point, life was starting to get extremely busy with retirement preparations and wrapping up projects. Life continued to be zany, but writing about it every day had become nearly impossible. I decided to take a breather and get back to it when life settled down. Besides, this book would become a novel of maladies if I kept going.

Although the impact of COVID has presented challenges to us, there have been many blessings that have come out of it. The biggest blessing has been the ability to slow down. Less commuting, no after-school activities, no after-school care, and just less overall distraction. We play more games, have more family meals together, and laugh more. We, as a family, realized we actually liked each other. Don't get me wrong, it's far from perfect (as you have read). We have also needed to respect that we need our own space. For the kids, going outside to play with their friends has been their mental sanity; TBG's stress relief is going for rides in his car; and for me it has been meditation and writing. As of this writing, we have not choked each other out. I'll be positive and say our method, thus far, is working.

Over this last year (my God, it's been over a year!), the kids enjoyed a COVID summer (thank God the pool stayed open); I went on terminal leave 1 August (surreal); and the kids started back to school remotely 24 August (a few tears were shed by all of us).

After surviving all the kids' meltdowns, fits, freak-outs, and fights with the Chromebook, TBG and I reluctantly decided to let them go back to school face-to-face after Christmas break. Three days later, I pulled Bianca out of school because her teacher was COVID-positive; two weeks later, one of her classmates tested positive; and three months later Bianca was COVID-positive. She and Brady won a two-week staycation….right over spring break.

On a positive note, I was officially retired from the military on 1 October...no retirement ceremony, no party; and in December, we bought our RV (freedom!), thus spurring a whole new set of adventures... or so we had hoped.

Life rarely seems to go as planned for us. Since I am not a very strict schedule kind of person, I'm pretty good at just going with it. Out of three scheduled RV trips, we made it to one, and our 2021 summer plans took a hard right. Our first trip was to Corpus Christi, where we learned the RV will protect us quite well during a major storm. Our second trip to San Angelo was kiboshed by the once-in-a-decade major southern Texas snowstorm. We seriously considered going with the thought the weather folks were probably overreacting. Ha! Week-long storm and a 12-gallon propane tank for heat; yeah, the joke would have been on us.

The third planned outing was squashed when Bianca picked up the COVID bug... the day before we were supposed to travel to northern Texas. Their entire spring break was spent in quarantine. Fortunately, she had a very mild case. But seriously, that was not what I had in mind for "together" time.

We kept our chins up (better than crying), and we were looking forward to being on the road for the summer, traveling around the U.S. Well, we'll be traveling; but instead of the whole Hoffmeyer clan in the RV, it will be Bianca and I on a road trip to New Hampshire, to take care of my parents after their matching hip replacements. Mom in June, Dad in July, and their 50th wedding anniversary in between. (Move over gold, titanium is the new 50th wedding anniversary gift.) Look out summer of 2022, this RV family is coming for you!

Vaccinations have rolled out, and the number of cases is finally dropping in the U.S. Globally, COVID is unfortunately still going strong in parts of the world, and we continue to send them lots of love and light. Still dealing with this virus over a year later is definitely not what any of us planned. We have to accept that it is what it is and be gratuitous for the little things, like finally giving another person a hug. Honestly, I don't think I can categorize a hug as a little thing right now. It's a big damn deal.

Bianca has learned both the fun and business side of book-writing and illustration. It's been a great project to work on together. I am so proud of her for sticking with it. (I'm so proud of myself for not losing my mind at times.)

Epilogue

We hope you enjoyed our tales of blissful chaos during COVID. Our goal was to give everyone a chuckle and hopefully realize you were not and are not alone. After all, laughter is truly the best medicine.

A Story Within A Story

A Story Within a Story

At the end of 1998, I was in the military, leaving my base in California and heading to my next assignment in Germany via a stop back home to New Hampshire. While I was there, I met up with three of my high school friends: Jen, Mary, and Stacey; and their daughters, Paige, Alex, and Madison, all around the age of 2. (I didn't have any children at the time.) They were adorable, and unbeknownst to me, 20+ years later they were all going to share their talents with me.

In 2017, I wrote my first book. Jen asked me if I was going to do an audiobook. I had no clue how to go about it. At the same time, Paige was studying at the Austin Art Institute and had all the professional equipment needed to develop the audiobook. Jen, having an amazing radio voice (she was a DJ "back in the day") read my book. and Paige did all the editing. That audiobook means the world to me.

In 2020, when I decided to turn the *Pandemic Parodies* Facebook posts into a book, I was trying to figure out how to give a little more visual to it. Without hesitation, our daughter, Bianca, excitedly volunteered to draw the pictures. She had never used a digital drawing pad before, and self-taught herself how to use Google draw. If you have never used a digital drawing pad before, give it a whirl and see how laborious it can be. Every picture in this book was her own creation. I couldn't be prouder.

Once the book was drafted and off to the editor, I needed to work on the book cover. Like divine intervention, Mary posted on

Facebook that Alex had a graphic design webpage. Without a thought, I immediately asked, "Does she do book covers?" I am proud to say that *Pandemic Parodies* is her first book cover, and she did an amazing job.

At the same time I was getting ready to meet with my editor on the draft, Stacey reached out to me. Madison had just graduated from college with her English degree, and was looking for jobs in the writing world. She asked if I knew of any possible opportunities. I mentioned this to my editor, and as fate would have it, his proofreader had just retired and he was looking for a new one. Madison now works for my editor; she was the proofreader of the *Pandemic Parodies*, and did a fantastic job. How cool is that!?

So please remember, investing in our children is investing into the future. Raise them well. You never know when your friend's snuggly, drippy-nose, drooly baby will become someone who impacts your life 20+ years from now in ways you never imagined.

Ladies, thank you all very much!

Dedication

To all the parents that have struggled juggling work, remote learning, and tears (yours and theirs); kept positive to alleviate fears; and laughed when it was all falling apart... this is for you.

To all the teachers, thank you for your commitment to our children. You can have your jobs back. You are our heroes; we bow to you. You need a raise... a big raise.

To all the kids, thank you for being your authentic, funny, worried selves, at a time you had little control. Your resiliency is amazing.

To all the healthcare workers, thank you from the bottom of my heart. There are no others who outrival your unwavering passion and dedication. You are our heroes.

Dedication

Acknowledgments

To my friends and family who continued to nudge me along to turn the *Pandemic Parodies* posts into this book... thank you.

Alex, thank you for an amazing book cover. You far surpassed my expectations and skill level (just look at my first book cover!).

Madison, it was an honor to have you be part of the development of this book. (Hope I didn't make your eyes bleed.)

Bianca, you make me proud every single day. Thank you for taking this project on with me. I love you.

Floyd, my super editor. Thank you for encouraging me to do the book. We are two books in together and I attribute much of my confidence to you.

Brian, Brady, Bianca, Amelia, Lilo and Puck, thank you for the laughs, antics, witty comebacks, and perpetual blissful chaos. There would be no book without you. Thank you for being part of my world. I love you.

Acknowledgments

About the Author and Illustrator

Donna Hoffmeyer, a Texas transplant, is originally from the small, quaint town of Colebrook in northern New Hampshire. She is a mom to Brady and Bianca, wife to Brian (a.k.a. The Big Guy), writer, blogger, podcaster, business owner, and a 21-year retired Air Force nurse. She retired at the rank of Lieutenant Colonel. Donna co-authored her first book in 2017, *Warrior to Patriot Citizen,* focusing on ensuring that service members are prepared for transition well before transition occurs. She also has her own mulitfacted business, REBel LLC, that publishes her own work and includes her blog, Taking Off The Armor, and podcast, Beyond the Frontline; both focused on all issues before, during, and after transition to civilian life; as well as, a business, The Transitioning Warrior, focused on veteran transition mentorship and consulting. You can contact her at rebelllc44@gmail.com or through her website www.rebel-llc.com.

Bianca Hoffmeyer is a Texas native, currently a 5th grader at Randolph Elementary, and has a true love for everything and anything art-related — writing, dancing, singing (often in the shower), painting, drawing, baking, learning languages, playing instruments, and crafts. It was her idea to draw pictures in the book. She self-taught herself to use Google Draw and penned every image in the book. She is an avid swimmer and student of Brazilian jiu jitsu, as well as an animal lover. She has two dogs (Amelia and Lilo), a cat (Puck) and is dreaming of (and begging for) a white-toe tree frog.